Better Homes and Gardens®

DIET RECIPES

© Copyright 1986 by Meredith Corporation, Des Moines, Iowa.
All Rights Reserved. Printed in the United States of America.
First Edition. First Printing.
Library of Congress Catalog Card Number: 85-71896
ISBN: 0-696-02192-7

BETTER HOMES AND GARDENS® BOOKS

Editor Gerald M. Knox
Art Director Ernest Shelton
Managing Editor David A. Kirchner
Copy and Production Editors James D. Blume, Marsha Jahns, Mary Helen Schiltz, Carl Voss

Food and Nutrition Editor Nancy Byal
Department Head, Cook Books Sharyl Heiken
Associate Department Heads Sandra Granseth, Rosemary C. Hutchinson, Elizabeth Woolever
Senior Foods Editors Julia Malloy, Marcia Stanley, Joyce Trollope
Associate Foods Editors Barbara Atkins, Linda Foley, Linda Henry, Lynn Hoppe, Jill Johnson, Mary Jo Plutt, Maureen Powers, Martha Schiel
Recipe Development Editor Marion Viall
Test Kitchen Director Sharon Stilwell
Test Kitchen Photo Studio Director Janet Pittman
Test Kitchen Home Economists Jean Brekke, Kay Cargill, Marilyn Cornelius, Jennifer Darling, Maryellyn Krantz, Lynelle Munn, Dianna Nolin, Marge Steenson, Cynthia Volcko

Associate Art Directors Linda Ford Vermie, Neoma Alt West, Randall Yontz
Assistant Art Directors Lynda Haupert, Harijs Priekulis, Tom Wegner
Senior Graphic Designers Mike Eagleton, Lyne Neymeyer, Stan Sams
Graphic Designers Mike Burns, Sally Cooper, Jack Murphy, Darla Whipple-Frain, Brian Wignall, Kimberly Zarley

Vice President, Editorial Director Doris Eby
Executive Director, Editorial Services Duane L. Gregg

President, Book Group Fred Stines
Director of Publishing Robert B. Nelson
Vice President, Retail Marketing Jamie Martin
Vice President, Direct Marketing Arthur Heydendael

Diet Recipes
Editor Maureen Powers
Copy and Production Editor Marsha Jahns
Graphic Designer Tom Wegner
Electronic Text Processor Donna Russell
Photographers Michael Jensen and Sean Fitzgerald
Food Stylists Marilyn Cornelius, Janet Pittman, Maria Rolandelli

On the cover
Terrific Taco Pie with Calorie-Trimmed Crust
(see recipes, page 108)

Our seal assures you that every recipe in *Diet Recipes*
has been tested in the Better Homes and Gardens® Test Kitchen.
This means that each receipe is practical and reliable, and meets
our high standards of taste appeal.

"**I**'m on a diet" is a familiar refrain. Whether you're a serious dieter or a casual calorie counter, it's important to get the most from the calories you consume. That's why you need dishes that not only fill you up and provide needed nutrients, but also taste terrific! Because main dishes provide the majority of the calories in a meal—and most of your daily protein requirements—they're the most important dishes in *any* diet.

The recipes in this book were chosen with those needs in mind. You'll find them long on variety and flavor, but short on calories. Take a look at *Diet Recipes*. Turn the page and start creating hearty soups, garden-fresh salads, delicate crepes, mouth-watering quiches, and much, much more. Dieting has never been so delicious!

Contents

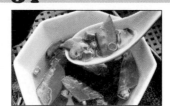

Tempting Casseroles

Look no further for slimming, quick-to-fix casseroles. Our recipes prove that hearty, one-dish meals don't need to be high in calories or time-consuming to prepare. Try one for supper tonight. In just minutes you'll have tantalizing results.

Salmon-Rice Bake

Salmon-Rice Bake

1   **10-ounce package frozen peas**
1   **15½-ounce can salmon, drained**
1   **7½-ounce can semicondensed cream of mushroom soup**
1   **soup can (1 cup) skim milk**
1   **4-ounce package (1 cup) shredded cheddar cheese**
¾   **cup quick-cooking rice**
2   **teaspoons minced dried onion**
¼   **teaspoon dried dillweed**

307 calories per serving

In a colander run hot water over peas for about 1 minute or until thawed (see photo 1). Drain peas well. Remove skin and bones from salmon (see photo 2). Break salmon into large chunks. In a 1½-quart casserole mix peas, soup, milk, cheese, uncooked rice, onion, and dillweed. Gently stir in salmon. Cover casserole (see photo 3). Bake in a 350° oven for 50 minutes. Remove the casserole from the oven. Let stand, covered, for 10 minutes.
Makes 6 servings.

1 To quickly thaw frozen vegetables, place them in a colander and rinse under hot tap water for about 1 minute.

2 Using your fingers, pull apart the sections of canned salmon, then remove the bones and skin, being careful to keep the fish in chunks. The chunks will make the finished dish more attractive.

3 Cover the casserole to keep food moist during baking. If your dish doesn't have a lid, use a piece of foil slightly larger than the top of the dish. Shape the foil over the dish, sealing the edges.

Turkey-Vegetable Casserole

The whole family will enjoy this homey casserole, never suspecting it's a diet recipe.

1 **10-ounce package frozen mixed vegetables**
2 **6-ounce packages sliced turkey luncheon meat**
1 **10¾-ounce can condensed cream of chicken soup**
1 **cup hot water**
¾ **cup quick-cooking barley**
1 **teaspoon poultry seasoning**
¼ **teaspoon onion powder**

247 calories per serving

In a colander run hot water over vegetables for about 1 minute or until thawed (see photo 1). Drain vegetables well. Place turkey in a stack, then cut it all at once into thin strips.

In a 2-quart casserole combine soup, water, barley, poultry seasoning, and onion powder. Stir in thawed vegetables and turkey. Cover the casserole (see photo 3). Bake in a 350° oven for 65 minutes, stirring once. Remove the casserole from the oven. Let stand, covered, for 10 minutes. Makes 6 servings.

10

Scrumptious Sandwiches

Ordinary sandwiches become extraordinary simply by changing the bread you use! Pick a pita pocket, a flour tortilla, or sliced whole wheat bread. Then, turn the page for an impressive display of scrumptious fillings.

Tangy Beef and Swiss Sandwiches

Tangy Beef and Swiss Sandwiches

½ cup plain low-fat yogurt
1 tablespoon snipped parsley
1 tablespoon finely shredded carrot
¼ teaspoon garlic salt *or* onion salt
⅛ teaspoon dried basil *or* tarragon,
   crushed
4 ounces thinly sliced cooked beef
4 ounces Swiss cheese
¼ cup coarsely chopped cucumber
¼ cup coarsely chopped tomato
¼ cup chopped green pepper
4 leaves leaf lettuce
½ cup alfalfa sprouts
4 slices whole wheat bread, 2 large
   pita bread rounds, *or* four 8-inch
   flour tortillas

190 calories per serving for filling

In a small bowl combine yogurt, parsley, carrot, garlic or onion salt, and basil or tarragon. Mix well, then cover and chill.

Cut beef and cheese into thin, matchlike strips (julienne strips). In a medium bowl mix beef, cheese, cucumber, tomato, and green pepper. Add yogurt mixture (see photo 1). Toss gently to coat. Prepare sandwiches using lettuce; sprouts; and bread (see photo 2), pita bread (see photo 3), or tortillas (see photo 4). Makes 4 servings.

1 Add the yogurt mixture to the beef and Swiss cheese mixture all at once. Gently toss the ingredients together until all of the beef and cheese mixture is coated. This careful stirring keeps the cheese from breaking into pieces.

2 Make open-face sandwiches by using four slices of whole wheat bread. Line each slice of bread with a lettuce leaf, then spoon the beef and Swiss cheese mixture onto the bread. Cut each sandwich in half diagonally with a sharp knife, as shown. Top each sandwich with some of the alfalfa sprouts. (258 calories per serving)

3 Create pita pocket sandwiches by cutting two large pita bread rounds in half crosswise with a knife or kitchen shears. If necessary, gently slip a knife into each pita pocket to loosen the sides so the pocket will open easily without tearing. Line each pocket with a lettuce leaf. Spoon the beef and Swiss cheese mixture into the pockets, as shown. Top each pita sandwich with some of the alfalfa sprouts. (230 calories per serving)

4 Assemble open-face tortilla sandwiches by using four 8-inch tortillas. Buy ready-to-use flour tortillas in the refrigerated section of the supermarket. Top each flour tortilla with a lettuce leaf. Spoon the beef and Swiss cheese mixture onto the tortillas. Top each tortilla with some of the alfalfa sprouts, as shown. (285 calories per serving)

Egg Salad Surprise

6 hard-cooked eggs, chopped
1 medium tomato, seeded and chopped
½ cup sliced celery
½ cup cubed sharp cheddar cheese
    (2 ounces)
1 4-ounce can chopped green
    chili peppers, drained
¼ cup dairy sour cream
1 tablespoon skim milk
¼ teaspoon salt
    Several dashes bottled hot pepper sauce
    Dash pepper
4 slices rye bread *or* wheat bread
4 leaves leaf lettuce

293 calories per serving

In a medium bowl combine eggs, tomato, celery, and cheese. For dressing, in a small bowl combine chili peppers, sour cream, milk, salt, pepper sauce, and pepper. Pour dressing over egg mixture, then toss gently to coat (see photo 1, page 12). Chill 2 to 3 hours. To make open-face sandwiches, line each bread slice with a lettuce leaf. Spoon egg mixture onto bread slices, then cut each sandwich diagonally with a knife (see photo 2, page 12). Serves 4.

To make pita sandwiches: Use two large *pita bread rounds*. Cut bread in half crosswise. Line each pita pocket with a lettuce leaf. Spoon egg mixture into pockets (see photo 3, page 13). Makes 4 servings. (265 calories per serving)

Cheese and Veggie Sandwiches

1½ cups low-fat cottage cheese, drained
¼ cup shredded carrot
¼ cup chopped green pepper,
    radish, *or* celery
½ teaspoon finely snipped chives
¼ cup dairy sour cream
4 slices whole wheat *or* white bread
2 tablespoons horseradish mustard
    Spinach leaves
4 slices tomato

188 calories per serving

In a medium bowl combine drained cheese; carrot; green pepper, radish, or celery; and chives. Add sour cream to cheese mixture (see photo 1, page 12). Stir to combine. To make open-face sandwiches, spread bread slices with horseradish mustard, then top with spinach leaves. Spoon cheese mixture onto bread slices. Top with a tomato slice. Cut each sandwich in half diagonally (see photo 2, page 12). Serves 4.

To make tortilla sandwiches: Use four 8-inch *flour tortillas*. Spread tortillas with horseradish mustard, then top with spinach leaves. Spoon cheese mixture onto tortillas. Top with a tomato slice. Makes 4 servings. (215 calories per serving)

Curried Turkeywiches

Curry gets its golden color from turmeric, one of 20 herbs and spices used in this seasoning blend.

2 cups diced cooked turkey *or* chicken (10 ounces)
1 medium apple, cored and chopped
¼ cup chopped green pepper
3 ounces Neufchâtel cheese, softened
½ teaspoon curry powder
2 tablespoons orange juice
4 large pita bread rounds
Bibb *or* leaf lettuce

261 calories per serving

In a medium bowl combine turkey or chicken, apple, and green pepper. To make dressing, in a small bowl combine cheese and curry powder, then stir in orange juice until mixture is smooth. Add dressing to turkey mixture, then toss gently to coat (see photo 1, page 12). Chill several hours. If necessary, stir in additional orange juice to make desired consistency. To make pita pockets, cut pita bread in half crosswise. Line each pocket with lettuce. Spoon turkey mixture into pockets (see photo 3, page 13). Serves 4.

To make tortilla sandwiches: Use four 8-inch *flour tortillas*. Top each tortilla with lettuce. Spoon turkey mixture onto tortillas. Makes 4 servings. (276 calories per serving)

Seaside Sandwiches

Using a 6½-ounce can of water-pack tuna in place of the crab slashes the cost without sacrificing flavor.

1 6-ounce package frozen crabmeat
2 hard-cooked eggs, chopped
½ cup chopped fresh spinach, endive, *or* romaine
½ cup chopped water chestnuts
1 tomato, peeled, seeded, and chopped
½ of a small cucumber, peeled, seeded, and chopped
⅓ cup dairy sour cream
¼ teaspoon salt
¼ teaspoon finely shredded lemon peel
4 8-inch flour tortillas

232 calories per serving

Thaw crabmeat. Flake crabmeat, then drain well in a strainer. Press crabmeat with the back of a spoon against the sides of the strainer to remove excess liquid. In a medium bowl combine crabmeat; eggs; spinach, endive, or romaine; water chestnuts; tomato; and cucumber. In a small bowl combine sour cream, salt, and lemon peel, then gently stir it into crab mixture (see photo 1, page 12). To make tortilla sandwiches, spoon crab mixture onto tortillas. Makes 4 servings.

To make open-face wheat sandwiches: Use four slices *whole wheat bread*. Spoon crab mixture onto bread slices. Cut each sandwich diagonally with a knife (see photo 2, page 12). Makes 4 servings. (204 calories per serving)

Refreshing Salads

Salads are a natural choice for dieters and anyone else looking for a light meal. Enhance your next salad with a homemade diet dressing that starts with our rich, creamy Salad Dressing Base. This tasty dressing base has less than *one-sixth* of the calories found in regular bottled mayonnaise!

Fruity Chicken Salad

Salad Dressing Base

1 tablespoon all-purpose flour
2 teaspoons sugar
1 teaspoon dry mustard
¾ cup skim milk
2 slightly beaten egg yolks
3 tablespoons vinegar

15 calories per tablespoon

In a 1-quart saucepan combine flour, sugar, mustard, and ½ teaspoon *salt*. Stir in milk gradually (see photo 1). Cook and stir until thickened and bubbly, then cook and stir 2 minutes more (see photo 2). Gradually stir some of the hot mixture into egg yolks (see photo 3). Return all to mixture in the saucepan. Return to a gentle boil, stirring constantly. Cook and stir 2 minutes more. Stir in vinegar. Place in a screw-top jar. Cover and chill. Store in the refrigerator for up to 1 week. Use in salad dressings or as a sandwich spread. Makes 1 cup.

Fruity Chicken Salad

1 cup Salad Dressing Base (see recipe, above)
1 teaspoon finely shredded orange peel
2 tablespoons orange juice
1 small cantaloupe
3 cups torn spinach
3 cups torn romaine
2½ cups diced cooked chicken
1½ cups strawberries, halved
¾ cup bias-sliced celery

184 calories per serving

For dressing, prepare Salad Dressing Base. Stir in orange peel and juice. Cover and chill. Remove seeds from cantaloupe, then scoop out balls to make about 1½ cups (see photo 4). In a large bowl mix melon, spinach, romaine, chicken, strawberries, and celery. Spoon mixture into six individual salad bowls. Drizzle some dressing over each (see photo 5). Serves 6.

1 Stir constantly as you gradually add the milk to the flour mixture. The milk and flour must be well combined to avoid lumps.

2 Cook mixture over medium-high heat till thickened and bubbly. Bubbles should break gently over the entire surface.

3 With a wire whisk or wooden spoon stir about ¼ cup of the hot mixture into the beaten egg yolks. Adding the egg yolks directly to the hot mixture would cook them too fast and cause curdling.

4 To make melon balls, scoop the fruit with a melon baller. Invert the melon baller and push it down into the fruit, rotating it to cut each ball.

5 Drizzle about 3 tablespoons of the orange-flavored salad dressing evenly over the top of each salad just before serving.

Tempting Tuna Salad

To quickly thaw the frozen loose-pack broccoli, see photo 1, page 8.

⅔ cup **Salad Dressing Base (see recipe, page 18)**
1½ teaspoons **Dijon-style mustard**
¼ teaspoon **celery seed**
1 cup **frozen chopped broccoli, thawed and drained**
½ cup **shredded cheddar cheese**
¼ cup **sliced pitted ripe olives**
1 **hard-cooked egg, chopped**
1 **6½-ounce can water-pack tuna, drained and flaked**
Leaf lettuce

213 calories per serving

For dressing, prepare Salad Dressing Base (see photos 1–3, page 18). In a bowl combine ⅔ *cup* of the base, mustard, and celery seed, then cover and chill.

In a large bowl combine broccoli, cheese, olives, and egg. Pour dressing over broccoli mixture and toss to coat. Carefully stir in tuna, then cover and chill. Serve on lettuce-lined salad plates. Makes 4 servings.

Cheese and Fruit Salad

½ cup **Salad Dressing Base (see recipe, page 18)**
1 tablespoon **honey**
½ teaspoon **poppy seed**
1 **pear, cored**
1 **apple, cored**
1 cup **seedless red *or* green grapes, halved**
3 ounces **Swiss cheese, cubed**
3 ounces **cheddar cheese, cubed**
Leaf lettuce

285 calories per serving

For dressing, prepare Salad Dressing Base (see photos 1–3, page 18). In a small bowl combine ½ *cup* of the base, honey, and poppy seed, then mix well. Cover and chill.

Slice pear and apple into thin wedges. In a large bowl combine pear, apple, grapes, and cheeses. Pour dressing over fruit-cheese mixture, then toss to coat. Serve in a lettuce-lined salad bowl. Makes 4 servings.

Beef Eater's Bounty

Use leftover roast beef or buy deli roast beef for this hearty beef salad.

1 cup **Salad Dressing Base (see recipe, page 18)**
½ cup **crumbled blue cheese**
¼ cup **dairy sour cream**
¼ teaspoon **coarsely ground pepper**
Dash bottled hot pepper sauce
½ pound **thinly sliced cooked beef**
6 cups **torn romaine lettuce**
1½ cups **fresh mushrooms, halved**
10 **cherry tomatoes, halved**
¼ cup **thinly sliced green onion**

203 calories per serving

For dressing, prepare Salad Dressing Base (see photos 1–3, page 18). In a small bowl combine base, *half* of the blue cheese, sour cream, pepper, and pepper sauce. Beat with a rotary beater until almost smooth. Stir in remaining blue cheese, then cover and chill.

Cut beef into thin, matchlike strips (julienne strips). In a large bowl combine beef, romaine, mushrooms, tomatoes, and onion. Spoon beef-vegetable mixture into individual salad bowls. Drizzle about ¼ *cup* of the dressing over each salad (see photo 5, page 19). Makes 6 servings.

Tropical Salmon Salad

To toast coconut, place the coconut in a shallow baking pan. Bake in a 350° oven for 5 to 10 minutes or till lightly browned, stirring once or twice.

½ cup Salad Dressing Base
   (see recipe, page 18)
1 8-ounce can crushed pineapple
   (juice pack)
⅛ teaspoon ground ginger
1 15½-ounce can salmon, drained
½ cup chopped water chestnuts
¼ cup chopped green pepper
   Leaf lettuce
¼ cup coconut, toasted

237 calories per serving

For dressing, prepare Salad Dressing Base (see photos 1–3, page 18). Drain pineapple, reserving 1 tablespoon juice. In a small bowl combine *½ cup* of the base, reserved pineapple juice, and ginger, then cover and chill.

Remove skin and bones from salmon (see photo 2, page 9). Flake salmon into a large bowl. Add drained pineapple, water chestnuts, and green pepper. Add dressing to salmon mixture and toss gently to coat. Cover and chill 2 hours.

Serve on four individual lettuce-lined salad plates. Sprinkle each salad with some of the coconut. Makes 4 servings.

Summer Fruit-Chicken Salad

½ cup Salad Dressing Base
   (see recipe, page 18)
2 tablespoons honey
1 tablespoon vinegar
1 teaspoon lemon juice
½ teaspoon curry powder
⅛ teaspoon ground ginger
2½ cups cubed cooked chicken
1½ cups thinly sliced celery
1 tablespoon thinly sliced green
   onion
3 medium nectarines
1½ cups dark sweet cherries,
¼ cup slivered almonds
   Leaf lettuce

241 calories per serving

For dressing, prepare Salad Dressing Base (see photos 1–3, page 18). In a small bowl combine *½ cup* of the base, honey, vinegar, lemon juice, curry powder, and ginger. Cover and chill. In a large bowl mix chicken, celery, and onion, then cover and chill. Chill nectarines and cherries.

Spread almonds in a single layer in a shallow baking pan. Toast nuts in a 350° oven for 10 to 12 minutes or till golden brown, stirring once.

Just before serving, pit and slice nectarines. Halve and pit cherries. Pour dressing over chicken mixture, then add nectarines, cherries, and almonds. Toss lightly to mix. Serve in a lettuce-lined bowl. Makes 6 servings.

Flavorful Simmered Meats

Slow-cook less tender cuts of meat to mouth-watering perfection. Simply trim away separable fat, brown the meat without oil, and then simmer in a flavorful liquid. Spicy Beef Stew is the perfect example of sensational eating. It's a rich beef stew, chock-full of colorful carrots, broccoli, and tomatoes. Indulge!

Spicy Beef Stew

Spicy Beef Stew

1 **pound beef round steak**
   Nonstick spray coating
½ **cup chopped onion**
1 **clove garlic, minced**
1 **16-ounce can tomatoes, cut up**
2 **cups water**
1 **10½-ounce can condensed beef broth**
1 **tablespoon chili powder**
½ **teaspoon ground cumin**
½ **teaspoon dried basil, crushed**
4 **large carrots**
1 **10-ounce package frozen cut broccoli**
2 **tablespoons cold water**
1 **tablespoon cornstarch**

160 calories per serving

Trim separable fat from meat (see photo 1). Cut meat into ¾-inch cubes. Spray a large saucepan with nonstick coating (see photo 2). Heat the saucepan. Cook meat, onion, and garlic in the saucepan over medium-high heat until meat is brown. Drain off fat. Stir in *undrained* tomatoes, water, broth, chili powder, cumin, and basil. Bring mixture to boiling; reduce heat. Cover and simmer for 1½ hours or until meat is tender.

Cut carrots into thin matchlike sticks (julienne strips). Stir carrots and broccoli into stew mixture, then cover and simmer for 8 to 10 minutes more or until carrots and broccoli are crisptender (see photo 3).

In a small bowl combine cold water and cornstarch (see photo 4). Stir into stew. Cook and stir until thickened and bubbly, then cook and stir for 2 minutes more. Makes 4 servings.

1 Trim away as much of the fat as possible from the meat to eliminate unnecessary calories. Use a sharp knife to cut off the separable fat—the fat that usually appears in a solid piece around the outside of the meat.

2 Before you begin heating the saucepan, Dutch oven, or skillet, spray it with a nonstick spray coating. Hold the can and the cooking utensil at arm's length and spray away from yourself so you don't inhale fumes.

3 To test the vegetables for tenderness, insert a fork into several of them. Select the stalkier and tougher vegetables for testing. Carrots and the stalk of the broccoli, for example, will not cook as quickly as the floweret portion of the broccoli.

When done, the vegetables should still be slightly crisp, but tender. This means that the fork will pierce the vegetables, but they will not feel mushy or fall apart.

4 Stir the cold water and cornstarch together until the cornstarch is dissolved. (If the mixture isn't used immediately, stir it again before using it, because the mixture will separate.) Slowly stir the cornstarch mixture into the hot stew. This technique keeps the cornstarch from lumping when added to the hot mixture.

Burgundy Beef

1	pound boneless beef top round steak, cut ½ inch thick
	Nonstick spray coating
1	cup coarsely shredded carrot
½	cup chopped onion
½	cup burgundy
½	cup water
1	clove garlic, minced
1	tablespoon cold water
1½	teaspoons cornstarch

176 calories per serving

Trim separable fat from steak (see photo 1, page 24). Cut meat into four pieces. Pound with a meat mallet until the meat is about ¼ inch thick (see photo 2, page 114). Sprinkle meat with salt and pepper. Spray a 10-inch skillet with nonstick coating (see photo 2, page 24). Heat the skillet. Cook meat quickly in skillet on both sides until meat is brown. Drain off fat.

Add carrot, onion, burgundy, ½ cup water, and garlic to the skillet. Bring mixture to boiling; reduce heat. Cover and simmer for 45 minutes or until meat is tender. Transfer meat to a serving platter and cover with foil to keep warm.

In a small bowl combine cold water and cornstarch (see photo 4, page 25). Stir mixture into cooking liquid. Cook and stir until thickened and bubbly, then cook and stir 2 minutes more. Serve over meat. Makes 4 servings.

Veal Stew

¾	pound veal stew meat
	Nonstick spray coating
1	small onion, cut into thin wedges
1	16-ounce can stewed tomatoes, cut up
1	6-ounce can tomato juice
½	teaspoon dried thyme, crushed
3	medium carrots, sliced ½ inch thick
1	medium turnip, peeled and coarsely chopped
1	tablespoon cornstarch
1	tablespoon cold water

221 calories per serving

Trim separable fat from stew meat (see photo 1, page 24). Cut meat into ¾-inch cubes. Spray a 3-quart saucepan with nonstick coating (see photo 2, page 24). Heat the saucepan. Cook meat and onion in the saucepan over medium-high heat until meat is brown. Drain off fat.

Add *undrained* tomatoes, tomato juice, and thyme to the saucepan. Bring mixture to boiling; reduce heat. Cover and simmer for 25 minutes. Stir in carrots and turnip. Cook for 25 to 30 minutes more or until meat and vegetables are tender (see photo 3, page 25).

In a small bowl combine cornstarch and cold water (see photo 4, page 25). Add mixture to stew. Cook and stir until mixture is thickened and bubbly, then cook and stir 2 minutes more. Makes 4 servings.

Saucy Steaks

Arrange the juicy steaks over hot noodles, then smother them with the delicious beer-cheese sauce. You'll wish you were always on a diet!

¾ pound beef round steak,
   cut ½ inch thick
   Nonstick spray coating
1 11-ounce can condensed cheddar
   cheese soup
¾ cup light beer
¾ teaspoon dried oregano, crushed
¼ teaspoon pepper
1 medium onion, sliced and separated
   into rings
3 ounces medium noodles

300 calories per serving

Trim separable fat from steak (see photo 1, page 24). Cut it into four serving-size pieces. Spray a 10-inch skillet with nonstick coating (see photo 2, page 24). Heat the skillet. Cook meat in the skillet on both sides until meat is brown. Drain off fat.

In a medium bowl combine soup, beer, oregano, and pepper. Pour soup mixture over steak, then top with onion. Cook, covered, for 1 hour or until meat is tender. Cook noodles according to package directions. Drain. Arrange noodles on a warm serving platter and place steaks atop noodles. Pour sauce over steaks and noodles. Makes 4 servings.

Lamb Chops and Vegetables

Adding a small amount of dried mint gives this lamb dish a distinctive, yet delicate flavor. If you have fresh mint, use 1 tablespoon of snipped leaves.

4 lamb leg sirloin chops, cut ¾ inch thick
   (1¼ pounds)
   Nonstick spray coating
   Salt
   Pepper
¼ cup water
2 teaspoons instant chicken
   bouillon granules
1 teaspoon dried mint, crushed
1½ cups frozen small whole onions
1 medium green pepper, cut into strips
2 medium tomatoes, cut into wedges
   Fresh mint sprigs (optional)

148 calories per serving

Trim separable fat from chops (see photo 1, page 24). Spray a 10-inch skillet with nonstick coating (see photo 2, page 24). Heat the skillet. Cook chops in the skillet on both sides. Drain off fat. Season chops lightly with salt and pepper. Stir in water, bouillon granules, and mint. Bring mixture to boiling; reduce heat. Cover and simmer for 20 to 25 minutes or until chops are almost tender.

Add onions and green pepper to the skillet. Simmer, covered, for 5 to 7 minutes more or until green pepper is crisp-tender. Add tomatoes and cook mixture, covered, for 3 minutes or until heated through. Garnish with mint sprigs, if desired. Makes 4 servings.

Tasty Stuffed Vegetables

Which of these delectably different stuffed vegetables should you try first? It's a tough decision. Whatever your choice, you'll find the result is the same—a whole meal tucked into one neat, edible package.

Pork-and-Spinach-Filled Vegetables

Pork-and-Spinach-Filled Vegetables

Press the thawed spinach between several layers of paper towels to thoroughly drain, so it won't water out during cooking and make the dish too wet.

⅔	**cup water**
⅓	**cup long grain rice**
¼	**cup sliced green onion**
1	**pound ground pork**
¼	**teaspoon garlic salt**
1	**10-ounce package frozen chopped spinach, thawed and well drained**
1	**7½-ounce can semicondensed cream of mushroom soup**
2	**medium tomatoes, peeled, seeded, and chopped**
½	**teaspoon ground sage**
⅛	**teaspoon pepper**
6	**medium green peppers, three 8-ounce zucchini (6 to 8 inches long), or 6 large tomatoes**
3	**tablespoons grated Parmesan cheese**

278 calories per serving for filling

In a small saucepan combine water, rice, and green onion. Bring mixture to boiling; reduce the heat to low. Cover with a tight-fitting lid and cook for 15 minutes. Don't lift the cover. Remove mixture from the heat and let it stand, covered, for 5 minutes.

Meanwhile, in a 10-inch skillet cook pork until it's brown. Drain off fat (see photo 1). Return meat to the skillet, then sprinkle meat with garlic salt. Add cooked rice, spinach, soup, chopped tomato, sage, and pepper to meat, then mix well.

Prepare vegetable shells using green peppers (see photo 2), zucchini (see photo 3), or tomatoes (see photo 4).

Sprinkle shells with salt, then place them in a 13x9x2-inch baking dish. Spoon filling into shells (see photo 5). Bake shells in a 350° oven for 25 minutes or until heated through. Top each with some of the cheese. Serves 6.

1 To thoroughly drain the fat from the cooked ground meat, transfer the meat to a colander placed over a bowl. Let the meat stand a few minutes to drain, then discard the fat that's accumulated in the bowl.

2 Cut the stem ends from the green peppers; remove the seeds. (If necessary, cut a thin slice from the pepper bottoms so they will stand up.) Chop the pepper tops to make ¼ cup, then stir it into the pork mixture. In a medium saucepan cook the peppers, covered, in a large amount of boiling water for 3 to 5 minutes. Remove the peppers and invert them on paper towels to drain. (294 calories per serving)

3 Cut zucchini in half lengthwise. Cut and scoop out the pulp, leaving a ¼-inch edge, as shown. Chop ½ cup pulp; stir it into the pork mixture. Place the shells, cut side down, in a 10-inch skillet with ½ cup water. Cover and simmer for 4 minutes. Remove the shells. Invert them on paper towels to drain. (291 calories per serving)

5 Stuff vegetable shells by lightly spooning the filling into the shells. Be careful to divide the filling (and calories) evenly.

4 Cut a thin slice from the stem end of each tomato. Scoop out the center with a spoon. Reserve the pulp for another use. Invert the tomatoes on paper towels to drain. (318 calories per serving)

Greek-Style Stuffed Tomatoes

Traditional Greek favorites appear in this savory fill-ing—lamb, eggplant, yogurt, raisins, and cinnamon.

1 **pound ground lamb**
½ **cup chopped onion**
1 **cup peeled and diced eggplant**
¾ **cup water**
¼ **cup bulgur wheat**
¼ **cup raisins**
¼ **cup snipped parsley**
1 **beaten egg**
½ **cup plain low-fat yogurt**
¼ **teaspoon ground cinnamon**
¼ **teaspoon ground nutmeg**
6 **large tomatoes**
⅓ **cup plain low-fat yogurt (optional)**

196 calories per serving

In a 10-inch skillet cook lamb and onion until meat is brown and onion is tender, then drain off fat (see photo 1, page 30). Add eggplant, water, bulgur wheat, raisins, and parsley. Bring mixture to boiling; reduce heat. Cover and sim-mer for 15 minutes, stirring occasionally. Re-move from the heat.

In a small bowl combine egg, ½ cup yogurt, cinnamon, and nutmeg, then mix well. Add to meat mixture and season to taste with salt.

Cut off stem end of tomatoes. Scoop out pulp (see photo 4, page 31). Invert shells on paper towels to drain. Reserve tops and pulp for an-other use. Sprinkle shells with salt, then place them in a 13x9x2-inch baking dish. Spoon lamb mixture into shells (see photo 5, page 31). Bake, covered, in a 350° oven for 20 to 25 minutes or until heated through. To serve, dollop each shell with some of the ⅓ cup yogurt, if desired. Makes 6 servings.

Ham-and-Rice-Stuffed Green Peppers

¾ **cup quick-cooking rice**
1½ **cups diced fully cooked ham (8 ounces)**
1 **8-ounce can tomato sauce**
1 **2½-ounce jar sliced mushrooms, drained**
1 **tablespoon snipped parsley**
1 **teaspoon Worcestershire sauce**
¼ **teaspoon chili powder**
   Dash bottled hot pepper sauce
4 **large green peppers**

205 calories per serving

Cook rice according to package directions. In a large bowl combine rice, ham, tomato sauce, mushrooms, parsley, Worcestershire sauce, chili powder, and pepper sauce, then mix well.

Remove tops from green peppers; set tops aside. Remove membrane and seeds from pep-pers (see photo 2, page 31). Cook peppers and tops in boiling water for 3 to 5 minutes; remove and invert on paper towels to drain. Sprinkle shells with salt, then place them in an 8x8x2-inch baking dish. Spoon ham mixture into shells (see photo 5, page 31). Place tops of peppers over mixture. Bake in a 350° oven for 20 to 25 minutes or until heated through. Serves 4.

Taco-Filled Zucchini Shells

For attractive individual servings, place the zucchini shells in six au gratin baking dishes.

1	pound lean ground beef
½	cup chopped onion
2	tablespoons chopped green pepper
1	clove garlic, minced
1	medium tomato, peeled, seeded, and chopped
2	tablespoons tomato paste
2	tablespoons water
1½	teaspoons chili powder
¼	teaspoon salt
¼	teaspoon ground red pepper
3	eight-ounce zucchini, 6 to 8 inches long
½	cup shredded cheddar cheese
	Shredded lettuce (optional)

190 calories per serving

In a 10-inch skillet cook beef, onion, green pepper, and garlic until beef is brown and vegetables are tender. Drain off fat (see photo 1, page 30). Stir in tomato, tomato paste, water, chili powder, salt, and red pepper.

Halve each zucchini lengthwise. Scoop out pulp, leaving a ¼-inch shell (see photo 3, page 31). Chop enough pulp to make ½ cup, then stir into beef mixture. Place shells, cut side down, in a skillet. Add ½ cup *water* and bring to boiling. Cover and simmer for 4 to 5 minutes or just until tender; remove and invert on paper towels to drain. Sprinkle shells with salt, then place them in a 13x9x2-inch baking dish. Spoon beef mixture into shells (see photo 5, page 31). Spoon excess filling around shells.

Cover and bake in a 350° oven for 25 to 30 minutes or until heated through. Sprinkle each shell with some of the cheese and lettuce, if desired. Makes 6 servings.

Turkey-Stuffed Tomato Shells

1½	cups diced cooked turkey *or* chicken
1	7½-ounce can semicondensed cream of mushroom soup
½	cup chopped celery
1	2½-ounce jar sliced mushrooms, drained
2	tablespoons chopped pimiento
1	tablespoon snipped parsley
¼	teaspoon dried thyme, crushed
4	large tomatoes
¼	cup shredded cheddar *or* Swiss cheese (1 ounce)

219 calories per serving

In a medium bowl combine turkey or chicken, soup, celery, mushrooms, pimiento, parsley, and thyme, then mix well.

Cut off stem ends of tomatoes. Scoop out pulp (see photo 4, page 31). Invert shells on paper towels to drain. Reserve tops and pulp for another use.

Sprinkle shells with salt, then place them in an 8x8x2-inch baking dish. Spoon turkey mixture into shells (see photo 5, page 31). Spoon any excess filling around shells. Bake, uncovered, in a 350° oven for 20 to 25 minutes or until heated through. Sprinkle each shell with some of the cheddar or Swiss cheese. Makes 4 servings.

Savory Soups

It's hard to resist the aroma and flavor of a piping hot bowl of soup, especially if it's homemade.

Whether you opt for an exotic Oriental-style soup or a hearty seafood chowder, you'll find these satisfying soups are worth the effort of starting from scratch. They're packed with flavor and trimmed of every possible calorie.

Oriental Soup

Chicken Stock

**Bony chicken pieces (backs, necks, and
    wings) from 2 chickens**
2 large stalks celery with leaves, cut up
2 carrots, cut up
1 large onion, cut up
2 sprigs parsley
1 bay leaf
½ teaspoon dried thyme, crushed
2 whole cloves

2 calories per cup

In a Dutch oven place chicken, celery, carrots, onion, parsley, bay leaf, thyme, cloves, ½ teaspoon *salt*, and ¼ teaspoon *pepper*. Add 6 cups *water*. Bring to boiling; reduce heat. Cover and simmer for 1¼ hours. Remove chicken and strain stock (see photo 1). Discard chicken, vegetables, and seasonings. Clarify stock, if desired (see tip box, page 39).

If using the stock hot, skim off fat (see photo 2). *Or,* chill stock for 6 to 8 hours and lift off fat (see photo 3). Makes 5½ cups.

Oriental Soup

4 cups Chicken Stock (see recipe, left)
**2 cups fresh pea pods *or* one 6-ounce
    package frozen pea pods, thawed**
**2 cups diced fully cooked ham
    (about 10 ounces)**
**1 cup sliced fresh mushrooms *or*
    one 4-ounce can sliced mushrooms,
    drained**
¼ cup sliced green onion
2 tablespoons rice wine vinegar (optional)

171 calories per serving

Prepare Chicken Stock. Clean fresh pea pods and remove strings, if necessary (see photo 4). Bias-slice pea pods in half crosswise. Set aside. In a 3-quart saucepan combine Chicken Stock, ham, and mushrooms. Bring to boiling; reduce heat. Cover and simmer for 4 to 5 minutes.

Stir in pea pods and green onion (see photo 5). Cook 2 to 3 minutes more or till pea pods are crisp-tender. Stir in vinegar, if desired. Ladle into soup bowls. Serves 4.

1 Use a double layer of cheesecloth to line a colander or large sieve. Place it over a large bowl. Strain the prepared stock by pouring it through the colander or sieve, as shown. Discard the bones, meat, vegetables, and seasonings caught by the cheesecloth.

2 If you want to use the stock right away, remove the fat while the stock is still hot. Use a metal spoon to skim off the oily liquid (fat) that rises to the top.

3 If time allows, make the stock ahead and chill it. When the fat solidifies, remove it by lifting it off with a spoon. Chilling the stock allows you to remove a larger amount of the fat more easily than you can when the stock is hot.

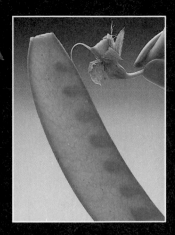

4 Remove the string from the pea pods by making a cut with a paring knife across the stem end of each pod and gently pulling down on the cut portion.

5 Peas pods are best when served crisp-tender. That's why they're added to the soup during the last few minutes of cooking.

Beef Stock (2 calories per cup): Prepare Chicken Stock (see recipe, page 36), *except* substitute 3 pounds *meaty beef soup bones* (neck, arm, shank, or marrow bones) for chicken pieces. Place bones in a large shallow roasting pan. Bake, uncovered, in a 450° oven for 30 minutes or till bones are well browned, turning occasionally. Drain off fat. Place browned bones in a Dutch oven. Continue recipe as directed.

Chicken-Barley Soup

5 cups Chicken Stock (see recipe, page 36)
¼ cup quick-cooking barley
1 bay leaf
1 teaspoon dried basil, crushed
¾ teaspoon salt
½ teaspoon dried savory, crushed
1 cup loose-pack frozen cut green beans, cut wax beans, *or* peas
1 cup thinly sliced carrots
2 cups cooked chicken, cut into ½-inch cubes

126 calories per serving

Prepare Chicken Stock (see photos 1–3, page 36). In a 3-quart saucepan combine Chicken Stock, barley, bay leaf, basil, salt, and savory. Add vegetables and bring to boiling; reduce heat. Cover and simmer for 12 to 15 minutes or till barley and vegetables are tender. Remove bay leaf. Add chicken, then heat through. Ladle into soup bowls. Makes 6 servings.

Shellfish Soup

3 cups Chicken Stock (see recipe, page 36)
3 medium carrots, cut into julienne strips
1 cup bias-sliced celery
1 cup frozen whole kernel corn
2 tablespoons snipped parsley
½ teaspoon dried basil, crushed
1 13-ounce can evaporated skimmed milk
1 8-ounce package frozen peeled and deveined shrimp
3 tablespoons cornstarch
3 tablespoons water
1 6-ounce can crabmeat, flaked, drained, and cartilage removed
½ teaspoon salt
⅛ teaspoon pepper

175 calories per serving

Prepare Chicken Stock (see photos 1–3, page 36). In a 3-quart saucepan combine Chicken Stock, carrots, celery, corn, parsley, and basil. Bring to boiling; reduce heat. Cover and simmer for 8 to 10 minutes or till vegetables are crisp-tender. Stir in milk and shrimp, then return to boiling. Combine cornstarch and water and stir into soup. Cook and stir till thickened and bubbly, then cook 2 minutes more. Stir in the crabmeat, salt, and pepper. Heat through. Ladle into soup bowls. Makes 6 servings.

Beefy Borscht

Borscht, the Slavic word for beet soup, has many flavor variations. We took the best ingredients from several versions and created our own rich borscht.

4 cups Beef Stock (see recipe, page 37)
   Nonstick spray coating
1 pound beef stew meat, trimmed of separable fat and cut into ¾-inch cubes
1 large turnip
2 medium beets *or* one 16-ounce can julienne beets, drained
1 carrot
¾ teaspoon salt
2 cups shredded cabbage

150 calories per serving

Prepare Beef Stock (see photos 1–3, page 36). Spray Dutch oven with nonstick coating. Cook meat in Dutch oven over medium-high heat till meat is brown. Drain off fat.

Meanwhile, peel turnip, beets, if needed, and carrot. Cut turnip and beets, if needed, into thin, matchlike strips. Cut carrot into ¼-inch bias slices (see photo 1, page 90). Add Beef Stock, turnip, beets, carrot, salt, and ¼ teaspoon *pepper* to meat. Bring to boiling; reduce heat. Cover and simmer for 50 minutes. Stir in cabbage. Cover and cook 10 minutes more or till vegetables and meat are tender. Ladle into soup bowls. Makes 6 servings.

Sausage and Cabbage Soup

We used smoked turkey sausage instead of pork sausage—it's lower in calories and just as flavorful.

4 cups Beef Stock (see recipe, page 37)
   Nonstick spray coating
1 large onion, chopped
½ cup thinly sliced celery
¼ cup chopped green pepper
1 clove garlic, minced
¾ pound fully cooked smoked turkey sausage, cut into ½-inch slices
2 medium potatoes, peeled and chopped (2 cups)
2 bay leaves
½ teaspoon salt
½ teaspoon caraway seed
¼ teaspoon pepper
5 cups coarsely shredded cabbage
   Parsley sprigs (optional)

215 calories per serving

Prepare Beef Stock (see photos 1–3, page 36). Spray a 3-quart saucepan with nonstick coating. In the saucepan combine onion, celery, green pepper, and garlic. Cook and stir over medium heat till vegetables are tender.

Stir in Beef Stock, sausage, potatoes, bay leaves, salt, caraway seed, and pepper. Bring mixture to boiling; reduce heat. Cover and simmer for 10 to 15 minutes or till potatoes are nearly tender. Remove bay leaves. Stir in cabbage. Cook, covered, for 5 to 10 minutes more or till the cabbage is crisp-tender. Ladle into soup bowls. Top each serving with parsley, if desired. Makes 6 servings.

Vegetable-Tofu Soup

1½ cups Chicken Stock (see recipe, page 36)
1   tablespoon minced dried onion
¼   teaspoon dried basil *or* oregano, crushed
2   cups loose-pack frozen mixed vegetables
1   10¾-ounce can condensed cream of celery *or* cream of mushroom soup
1½ cups skim milk
1   8-ounce package tofu (fresh bean curd), drained and cut into ½-inch cubes
¾   cup shredded American cheese

261 calories per serving

Prepare Chicken Stock (see photos 1–3, page 36). In a 3-quart saucepan combine Chicken Stock, onion, and basil or oregano. Bring to boiling. Stir in vegetables and return to boiling; reduce heat. Cover and simmer for 5 minutes. Stir in soup. Gradually add milk, then bring to boiling. Reduce heat. Add tofu and cheese and stir gently till cheese melts. Ladle into soup bowls. Makes 4 servings.

Clarifying Stock

Don't be alarmed if your home-made stock is cloudy even after straining. For a clear, rich-looking stock, you need to clarify it.

First, in a large saucepan stir together ¼ cup *cold water*, 1 *egg white*, and 1 *crushed eggshell*. Then, add the strained stock and bring it to boiling. Remove from the heat and let stand 5 minutes. Strain stock again through a colander or sieve lined with several layers of damp cheesecloth.

Elegant Poached Entrées

Tantalize your taste buds with these tempting entrées. Poaching (simmering food in a moderate amount of liquid) lends itself to low-calorie cooking. By using a liquid instead of cooking oil or fat, and the seasonings of your choice, you can keep calories under control. It doesn't matter if you prefer a fiery Mexican accent or a subtly sweet Hawaiian flavor. Simply change the character of the dish by varying the cooking liquid and seasonings.

Eggs Olé

Eggs Olé

4 6-inch flour tortillas
**2 large tomatoes, peeled, cored,
     and chopped**
1 8-ounce can tomato sauce
**1 4-ounce can green chili peppers,
     rinsed, seeded, and chopped**
2 teaspoons minced dried onion
¼ teaspoon dried oregano, crushed
**1 cup chopped cooked chicken *or* turkey
     Nonstick spray coating**
4 eggs

286 calories per serving

Brush one tortilla lightly with water to make it more pliable. Press it into an ovenproof 10-ounce casserole, shaping tortilla to fit the casserole (see photo 1). Repeat with remaining tortillas. Place casseroles in a shallow baking pan. Bake in a 350° oven for 15 to 20 minutes or just till tortillas are crisp. Cool on a wire rack; remove tortillas from casseroles.

For sauce, in a medium saucepan combine tomatoes, tomato sauce, chili peppers, onion, and oregano. Bring to boiling; reduce heat. Boil gently, uncovered, for 10 minutes or till desired consistency. Add chicken or turkey, then heat through. Keep warm.

To poach eggs, spray a 10-inch skillet with non-stick coating. Add enough water to half-fill the skillet (see photo 2). Bring water to boiling; reduce heat to simmering. Break an egg into a sauce dish. Carefully slide egg into water (see photo 3). Repeat with remaining eggs so each has about equal space in the skillet.

(For perfectly round poached eggs, place a metal egg ring in the simmering water. Slip egg into center of the ring. As soon as egg white sets, remove the ring.) Smooth edges of eggs during cooking by using a spoon to gently pull away any strings of egg white (see photo 4). Simmer, uncovered, for 3 to 5 minutes or till eggs are desired doneness.

Spoon a scant *½ cup* of sauce into *each* tortilla bowl, then place an *egg* in *each* tortilla bowl (see photo 5). Sprinkle with salt, if desired. Top with remaining sauce. Makes 4 servings.

1 To make a tortilla bowl, brush the tortilla lightly with water to keep it from breaking or cracking. The slightly moist tortilla will be more pliable so you can shape it easily. Shape the tortilla in a ruffle to fit a 10-ounce casserole, as shown.

2 Pour enough water or other cooking liquid into the skillet so that it is half full. This is usually about 1 inch of liquid.

5 Lift the cooked eggs out of the poaching liquid with a slotted spoon, draining well. Carefully place each egg into a tortilla bowl atop the sauce mixture.

3 Carefully slide the egg into the simmering liquid, holding the lip of the dish as close to the liquid as possible.

4 To make the eggs more attractive, use a slotted spoon to pull away any strings of the egg white that form while the eggs are cooking.

Hawaiian Chicken

Juice-pack pineapple tastes like fresh pineapple and has 50 calories less per cup than syrup-pack pineapple.

2 **whole medium chicken breasts (about 1½ pounds total), halved lengthwise**
1 **8-ounce can pineapple chunks *or* tidbits (juice pack)**
⅓ **cup orange juice**
2 **tablespoons soy sauce**
½ **teaspoon minced dried onion**
2 **teaspoons cornstarch**
2 **teaspoons cold water**

191 calories per serving

Remove and discard skin from chicken. Drain pineapple, reserving liquid. In a 10-inch skillet combine the reserved liquid, orange juice, soy sauce, and onion (see photo 2, page 42). Bring to boiling. Add chicken, then reduce heat. Cover and simmer for 25 to 30 minutes or till chicken is tender, turning once. Transfer chicken to a warm platter and keep warm.

For sauce, stir together cornstarch and water (see photo 4, page 25). Add to cooking liquid. Cook and stir till thickened and bubbly. Add pineapple, then cook and stir 2 minutes more. Spoon sauce over chicken. Makes 4 servings.

Zesty Chicken

2 **whole medium chicken breasts (about 1½ pounds total), halved lengthwise**
1 **cup vegetable juice cocktail**
¼ **cup chopped green pepper**
¼ **cup chopped onion**
1 **clove garlic, minced**
½ **teaspoon dried oregano, crushed**
   Dash bottled hot pepper sauce
1 **tablespoon cornstarch**
1 **tablespoon cold water**

172 calories per serving

Remove and discard skin from chicken. In a 10-inch skillet combine vegetable cocktail, green pepper, onion, garlic, oregano, and pepper sauce (see photo 2, page 42). Bring to boiling. Add chicken, then reduce heat. Cover and simmer for 25 to 30 minutes or till chicken is tender. Transfer chicken to a platter and keep warm.

For sauce, stir together cornstarch and cold water (see photo 4, page 25). Add to cooking liquid in skillet. Cook and stir till thickened and bubbly, then cook and stir 2 minutes more. Spoon sauce over chicken. Makes 4 servings.

Poached Halibut in Tangy Lime Sauce

4 **4-ounce fresh *or* frozen small halibut steaks (1 pound)**
½ **teaspoon finely shredded lime peel**
3 **tablespoons lime juice**
¼ **teaspoon dried rosemary, crushed**
½ **cup plain low-fat yogurt**
1 **tablespoon all-purpose flour**

180 calories per serving

Thaw fish, if frozen. In a 10-inch skillet combine lime peel, lime juice, rosemary, 1 cup *water,* ¼ teaspoon *salt,* and ⅛ teaspoon *pepper* (see photo 2, page 42). Add fish and bring to boiling; reduce heat. Cover and simmer for 8 to 10 minutes or till fish flakes easily with a fork (see photo 3, page 85). Transfer fish to a platter, leaving cooking liquid in the skillet. Keep fish warm.

For sauce, bring cooking liquid to boiling. Boil 5 minutes or till reduced to ½ cup. Reduce heat. In a small bowl combine yogurt and flour. Stir about *half* of the hot mixture into yogurt mixture, then return all to hot mixture. Cook and stir till thickened and bubbly, then cook and stir 1 minute more. Spoon sauce over fish. Garnish with lime slices and parsley, if desired. Serves 4.

Poached Fish with Lemon-Dill Sauce

If you don't have a fish poacher, use a large roasting pan. Wrap the fish in cheesecloth, then lay the fish on two wide strips of doubled foil in the pan. (The strips should be long enough to allow you to lift the fish.) When the fish is cooked, use the foil strips to remove the fish from the roasting pan.

1 **3-pound fresh *or* frozen dressed whiting *or* red snapper**
1 **cup water**
1 **cup dry white wine**
½ **teaspoon salt**
⅛ **teaspoon pepper**
½ **lemon, cut into wedges**
1 **bay leaf**
1 **tablespoon all-purpose flour**
½ **cup dairy sour cream**
1 **teaspoon fresh snipped dillweed *or* ¼ teaspoon dried dillweed**

253 calories per serving

Thaw fish, if frozen. Place fish on a large piece of cheesecloth, then fold cloth over fish. Place on a rack in a poaching pan. Add water, wine, salt, and pepper (see photo 2, page 42). Squeeze lemon wedges over fish, then add lemon wedges and bay leaf to poaching liquid. Bring to boiling; reduce heat. Cover and simmer for 25 to 30 minutes or till fish flakes easily with a fork (see photo 3, page 85). Remove fish from pan and keep warm. Strain and reserve ½ cup of the cooking liquid.

For sauce, in a small saucepan stir flour into sour cream. Stir in reserved liquid and dillweed. Cook and stir till thickened and bubbly, then cook and stir 1 minute more.

Pull cloth away from fish and discard, then remove and discard skin. Transfer fish to a serving platter using two metal spatulas. Top with some of the sauce and pass the remainder. Serves 6.

Poached Eggs with Shrimp Sauce

1 **tablespoon butter *or* margarine**
2 **teaspoons cornstarch**
⅛ **teaspoon dried tarragon, crushed**
  Dash pepper
⅔ **cup skim milk**
1 **4½-ounce can shrimp, rinsed and drained**
1 **10-ounce package frozen chopped spinach**
  Nonstick spray coating
4 **eggs**
2 **tablespoons shredded Swiss cheese**

194 calories per serving

For sauce, in a small saucepan melt butter or margarine. Stir in cornstarch, tarragon, and pepper. Add milk all at once. Cook and stir over medium heat till thickened and bubbly, then cook and stir 2 minutes more. Stir in shrimp and heat through. Keep sauce warm.

Cook spinach according to package directions. Meanwhile, to poach eggs, spray a 10-inch skillet with nonstick coating. Add enough water to half-fill the skillet, about 1 inch (see photo 2, page 42). Bring to boiling. Reduce heat to simmering. Break an egg into a sauce dish. Carefully slide egg into water, holding lip of the dish as close to water as possible (see photo 3, page 43). Repeat with remaining eggs so each has about equal space in the skillet. (For perfectly round eggs, place a metal egg ring in the simmering water. Slip egg into center of the ring. As soon as egg white sets, remove the ring.) Smooth edges of eggs during cooking by using a spoon to gently pull away any strings of egg white (see photo 4, page 43). Simmer, uncovered, for 3 to 5 minutes or till desired doneness.

Thoroughly drain spinach. Spoon spinach onto four individual plates. Lift eggs out of water using a slotted spoon and place an egg atop spinach on each plate. Season eggs lightly with salt. Spoon sauce over eggs. Sprinkle each serving with cheese. Makes 4 servings.

Tantalizing Broiled Meats

Finding a quick way to prepare dazzling dishes is important with today's busy life-styles. That's where broiling comes in—it's fast and easy.

Broiling offers another bonus—it uses no added fat. And, the fat that cooks out of the food is left behind in the broiler pan.

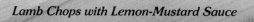
Lamb Chops with Lemon-Mustard Sauce

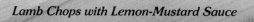

Lamb Chops with Lemon-Mustard Sauce

Elegant enough for company; low-calorie enough to please everyone.

4 lamb leg sirloin chops, cut ¾ inch thick (1¼ pounds)
½ teaspoon lemon pepper
½ teaspoon dry mustard
⅓ cup chicken broth
1 teaspoon cornstarch
2 tablespoons Dijon-style mustard
¼ teaspoon finely shredded lemon peel
1 tablespoon lemon juice
⅛ teaspoon dried oregano, crushed
1 clove garlic, minced
Fresh herb sprigs (optional)

142 calories per serving

Trim separable fat from chops (see photo 1, page 24). In a small bowl combine lemon pepper and dry mustard, then rub mixture into chops (see photo 1). Place chops on an unheated rack in a broiler pan. Broil 3 to 4 inches from the heat for 5 to 6 minutes (see photo 2). Turn chops (see photo 3). Broil 3 to 4 minutes more or till desired doneness (see photo 4).

Meanwhile, for sauce, in a 1-quart saucepan combine chicken broth and cornstarch. Stir in Dijon-style mustard, lemon peel, lemon juice, oregano, and garlic. Cook and stir till thickened and bubbly, then cook and stir 2 minutes more. Serve sauce over chops. Garnish with herbs, if desired. Makes 4 servings.

1 Rub the herb mixture into both sides of each lamb chop with your fingers.

2 Place the chops on an unheated rack in a broiler pan so that the surface of the chops is 3 to 4 inches from the heat source, as shown. Usually the door of an electric range needs to be ajar while the broiler is in use, but the door on a gas range is closed. Read the manufacturer's directions for your range to be sure.

3 Use tongs or a metal spatula instead of a fork to carefully turn each chop, as shown. Forks pierce meat, causing the loss of flavorful juices.

4 Test the lamb chops for doneness by making a small slit in the center of one of the chops. A medium-done chop will have a pink center; a well-done chop will be gray. For medium doneness, allow 6 minutes per side for ¾-inch chops.

Pineapple-Ham Kabobs

¾ pound fully cooked boneless ham
1 8-ounce can pineapple slices
    (juice pack)
1 medium green pepper, cut into squares
4 spiced crab apples (optional)
1 tablespoon honey
½ teaspoon cornstarch
¼ teaspoon ground cinnamon

204 calories per serving

Trim separable fat from ham (see photo 1, page 24). Cut ham into ¾-inch cubes. Drain pineapple slices, reserving juice. Quarter pineapple slices. On four long or eight short skewers alternately thread ham, pineapple, and green pepper. Place a crab apple at the end of each kabob, if desired.

For sauce, in a small saucepan combine reserved pineapple juice, honey, cornstarch, and cinnamon. Cook and stir till slightly thickened and bubbly, then cook and stir 2 minutes more. Baste kabobs generously with some sauce.

Place kabobs on an unheated rack in a broiler pan. Broil kabobs 4 inches from heat for 5 minutes (see photo 2, page 48). Brush occasionally with sauce. Turn kabobs and broil about 5 minutes more, brushing with sauce occasionally. Brush with remaining sauce before serving. Makes 4 servings.

Orange-Ginger Lobster

To clean your broiler pan more easily, let it soak for a few minutes in hot soapy water.

4 8-ounce frozen lobster tails
½ teaspoon finely shredded orange peel
½ cup orange juice
1 teaspoon cornstarch
⅛ teaspoon ground ginger
1 tablespoon butter *or* margarine

150 calories per serving

Partially thaw lobster. Use a sharp, heavy knife to cut through center of hard top shell. Cut through meat, but not through undershell. Pull tail open, butterfly-style, so meat is on top.

Place tails on an unheated rack in a broiler pan, cut side up. Broil about 5 inches from the heat for 12 to 15 minutes (see photo 2, page 48). Lobster should lose its translucency and flake easily when tested with a fork (see photo 3, page 85). Loosen meat from shell by inserting a fork between shell and meat.

Meanwhile, for dipping sauce, in a 1-quart saucepan combine orange peel, orange juice, cornstarch, and ginger. Cook and stir till thickened and bubbly, then cook and stir 2 minutes more. Stir in butter or margarine till melted. Serve sauce with lobster. Makes 4 servings.

Cheese-Stuffed Burgers

Mozzarella cheese has only 79 calories in 1 ounce, but you also can use Swiss cheese (105 calories) or cheddar cheese (113 calories).

    1 beaten egg
    2 tablespoons fine dry bread crumbs
    1 tablespoon water
    ¼ teaspoon garlic salt
    ¼ teaspoon dried thyme, crushed
       Dash pepper
    1 pound lean ground beef
    ¼ cup shredded mozzarella cheese
          (1 ounce)
    1 tablespoon snipped parsley
    1 small tomato, thinly sliced

245 calories per serving

In a medium bowl combine egg, bread crumbs, water, garlic salt, thyme, and pepper. Add beef and mix well. Shape beef mixture into eight ¼-inch-thick patties.

In a small bowl combine cheese and parsley. Spoon cheese mixture onto *four* patties. Top with remaining patties, then press edges to seal.

Place burgers on an unheated rack in a broiler pan. Broil 3 inches from the heat for 4 minutes (see photo 2, page 48). Turn patties with a metal spatula (see photo 3, page 49). Broil 4 to 5 minutes more or till desired doneness. Top burgers with tomato slices. Makes 4 servings.

South Seas Steak Pinwheels

Kiwi fruit is lemon-shaped with soft, fuzzy brown skin and delicate green fruit.

    ¾ pound boneless beef top round
          steak, cut ½ inch thick
    1 papaya, peeled and seeded
    1 small banana, finely chopped
    2 teaspoons lemon juice
       Dash ground nutmeg
    1 kiwi fruit, peeled and cut into
          thin slices

159 calories per serving

Trim separable fat from meat (see photo 1, page 24). Pound to ⅛-inch thickness (see photo 2, page 114). Sprinkle with salt and pepper. Finely chop enough papaya to measure ½ cup. Slice the remainder for garnish and set sliced papaya aside. In a small bowl combine chopped papaya, banana, lemon juice, and nutmeg. Spread fruit mixture over meat. Roll up jelly-roll style. Secure with wooden toothpicks. Cut crosswise into four slices.

Place meat on an unheated rack in a broiler pan. Broil meat 3 to 4 inches from the heat for 5 to 6 minutes (see photo 2, page 48). Carefully turn meat with a metal spatula (see photo 3, page 49). Broil 4 to 5 minutes more or till meat is desired doneness. Garnish meat with kiwi fruit and sliced papaya. Makes 4 servings.

Perfect Pasta

Now it's easy to eat great-tasting pasta dishes while watching your weight. The key to slimming success is low-calorie sauces.

Surprisingly, pasta isn't the calorie culprit. It's the rich, high-calorie sauces that make pasta dishes off-limits to dieters. Try any of the exciting recipes in this section and you can treat yourself to pasta as often as you please.

Vegetable Carbonara

Vegetable Carbonara

Often, green noodles are called spinach noodles on the package. If you can't find them at the supermarket, substitute regular noodles.

4 ounces green noodles
1 8-ounce package tofu (fresh bean curd)
1 carrot
¼ cup water
1 medium zucchini, halved lengthwise and
     sliced ¼ inch thick
1 cup sliced fresh mushrooms
¼ cup snipped parsley
¼ teaspoon salt
¼ teaspoon dried basil, crushed
2 slightly beaten eggs
⅓ cup grated Parmesan cheese

245 calories per serving

Cook noodles according to package directions; test for doneness (see photo 1). Drain noodles and keep warm (see photo 2). Meanwhile, drain tofu (bean curd). Wrap tofu in a double thickness of cheesecloth or paper towels, pressing gently to extract as much moisture as possible. Cut into ½-inch cubes (see photo 3).

Cut carrot into thin, matchlike strips (julienne strips). In a 10-inch skillet bring carrot and water to boiling; reduce heat to medium-high. Cover and cook for 3 minutes. Stir in tofu, zucchini, mushrooms, parsley, salt, and basil (see photo 4). Cover and cook about 7 minutes more or till zucchini is tender. Drain.

In a small bowl combine eggs and cheese. Add hot noodles to the skillet and toss with vegetables, then remove skillet from heat. Immediately add egg mixture to the skillet, then toss well to coat (see photo 5). Serves 4.

1 Near the end of the cooking time, test the pasta frequently for doneness by cutting with a fork or biting into a piece. When it's done, the pasta should be tender but still slightly firm. Italians call this *al dente* (to the tooth).

2 When the pasta tests done, immediately turn it into a colander over a sink and drain, being careful to avoid the hot steam. Give it a couple of shakes to help remove excess moisture. Keep the pasta warm after draining by placing the colander over a pot of hot water. Or, return the pasta to the pot and cover. Place the pot in a warm oven for a while.

3 After thoroughly draining tofu, use a serrated knife to make lengthwise cuts about ½ inch apart. Then, cut the strips crosswise to make cubes.

4 Add the tofu cubes, zucchini, mushrooms, parsley, salt, and basil to the skillet with the cooked carrots. Push the vegetables off the cutting board and into the skillet with a spatula so the hot liquid does not splash and hit your arm.

5 Toss the egg and Parmesan cheese mixture with the hot mixture in the skillet immediately, as shown. A wooden pasta fork and spatula works particularly well. Or, use two spoons. This tossing distributes the egg and cheese mixture, evenly coating the pasta and vegetables. Heat from the hot mixture will quickly cook the eggs.

Fettuccine with Clam Sauce

Prefer fresh clams? Try using 1 pint of shucked clams, chopped, in place of canned ones.

6 ounces fettuccine, green noodles,
    or spaghetti
2 6½- *or* 7½-ounce cans minced clams
1 cup thinly sliced carrots
1¾ cups skim milk
3 tablespoons cornstarch
½ cup sliced green onion
½ cup shredded Swiss cheese (2 ounces)
2 tablespoons chopped pimiento
¼ teaspoon salt
¼ teaspoon dried dillweed
    Dash pepper
    Snipped parsley (optional)

238 calories per serving

Cook fettuccine, green noodles, or spaghetti according to package directions; test for doneness (see photo 1, page 54). Drain the pasta and keep warm (see photo 2, page 54).

Meanwhile, for sauce, drain clams, reserving liquid. Set clams aside. In a 2-quart saucepan combine reserved liquid and carrots. Bring to boiling; reduce heat. Cover and simmer for 6 to 8 minutes or till tender. Stir together milk and cornstarch (see photo 4, page 25). Add all at once to carrot mixture. Add green onion. Cook and stir till thickened and bubbly, then cook and stir 2 minutes more.

Stir in clams, cheese, pimiento, salt, dillweed, and pepper, then heat through. Ladle clam sauce over pasta on a serving platter. Garnish with parsley, if desired. Makes 6 servings.

Scallops Italian

¾ pound fresh *or* frozen scallops
4 ounces linguine *or* spaghetti
    Nonstick spray coating
½ cup sliced celery
¼ cup chopped onion
1 clove garlic, minced
1 8-ounce can tomatoes, cut up
1 8-ounce can tomato sauce
1 3-ounce can sliced mushrooms, drained
¼ teaspoon dried rosemary, crushed
¼ teaspoon dried thyme, crushed
⅛ teaspoon salt
2 tablespoons snipped parsley
4 teaspoons cornstarch
1 tablespoon cold water

257 calories per serving

Thaw scallops, if frozen. Cut any large scallops in half and set aside. Cook linguine or spaghetti according to package directions; test for doneness (see photo 1, page 54). Drain pasta and keep warm (see photo 2, page 54).

Meanwhile, spray a 2-quart saucepan with nonstick coating. For sauce, in the saucepan cook celery, onion, and garlic till onion is tender. Stir in *undrained* tomatoes, tomato sauce, mushrooms, rosemary, thyme, and salt. Bring to boiling; add scallops and parsley. Return to boiling; reduce heat. Cover and simmer for 4 to 5 minutes or till scallops are nearly opaque.

Combine cornstarch and water (see photo 4, page 25). Stir cornstarch mixture into tomato mixture. Cook and stir till thickened and bubbly, then cook and stir 2 minutes more. Serve sauce over hot linguine or spaghetti on individual plates. Makes 4 servings.

Beefy Vegetable-Sauced Pasta

4	ounces fine *or* medium noodles
¾	pound lean ground beef
¼	cup chopped onion
¼	cup chopped green pepper
1½	cups thinly sliced cauliflower flowerets
1	10½-ounce can tomato puree
1	8-ounce can tomatoes, cut up
¼	cup snipped parsley
1	teaspoon dried oregano, crushed
½	teaspoon salt
¼	teaspoon dried basil, crushed
⅛	teaspoon garlic powder

305 calories per serving

Cook noodles according to package directions; test for doneness (see photo 1, page 54). Drain noodles and keep warm (see photo 2, page 54).

Meanwhile, for sauce, in a 10-inch skillet cook beef, onion, and green pepper till meat is brown and vegetables are tender, then drain off fat (see photo 1, page 30). Stir in cauliflower, tomato puree, *undrained* tomatoes, parsley, oregano, salt, basil, and garlic powder. Bring to boiling; reduce heat. Cover and simmer for 15 to 20 minutes or till the cauliflower is crisp-tender. Ladle sauce over noodles on a serving platter. Makes 4 servings.

White Lasagna

Enjoy this Northern Italian-style lasagna that features a rich white sauce in place of the traditional Southern-style tomato sauce.

4	ounces lasagna noodles (6 noodles)
1	10-ounce package frozen chopped broccoli
2	cups skim milk
2	tablespoons cornstarch
1	tablespoon minced dried onion
1½	cups diced fully cooked ham (½ pound)
½	teaspoon Italian seasoning, crushed
1	cup low-fat cottage cheese
1	cup shredded mozzarella cheese (6 ounces)

284 calories per serving

Cook lasagna noodles according to package directions; test for doneness (see photo 1, page 54). Drain noodles (see photo 2, page 54). Rinse noodles with cold water.

Meanwhile, cook broccoli according to package directions; drain well. Set aside. For sauce, in a medium saucepan combine milk, cornstarch, and onion. Cook and stir till thickened and bubbly, then cook and stir 2 minutes more. Stir in broccoli, ham, and Italian seasoning.

Place *2 tablespoons* of the sauce on the bottom of a 10x6x2-inch baking dish, then spread evenly. Place *two* of the lasagna noodles in baking dish. Spread noodles with *half* of the cottage cheese. Add *one-third* of sauce and mozzarella. Repeat noodle, cottage cheese, sauce, and mozzarella layers, then top with remaining noodles, sauce, and mozzarella.

Bake in a 375° oven for 30 to 35 minutes or till heated through. (*Or,* assemble and chill for up to 24 hours. Bake 45 to 50 minutes or till heated through.) Let stand 10 minutes before serving. Makes 6 servings.

Delectable Microwave Entrées

For a fast, efficient way to create spectacular low-calorie meals, put your microwave to work. Relish the flavors of piquant Pepper Steak, Quick Beef Stew, or Hot Turkey Salad. They're proof that the microwave oven can do some serious figuring in your diet plans.

Pepper Steak

Pepper Steak

¾ **pound beef top round steak**
1 **teaspoon grated gingerroot**
2 **tablespoons soy sauce**
2 **tablespoons dry sherry**
2 **teaspoons cornstarch**
1 **teaspoon instant beef bouillon granules**
1 **large green pepper, cut into strips**
1 **small tomato, cut into thin wedges**
2 **cups hot cooked noodles**

229 calories per serving

Trim separable fat from meat (see photo 1, page 24). Partially freeze meat. Thinly slice meat across the grain into strips (see photo 1). Place in a 2-quart nonmetal casserole. Micro-cook, covered, on 100% power (HIGH) for 4 to 5 minutes or till no longer pink, stirring twice (see photo 2).

Grate gingerroot (see photo 3). Mix gingerroot, soy sauce, sherry, cornstarch, bouillon granules, and 2 tablespoons *cold water*. Stir into beef. Stir in green pepper. Micro-cook, uncovered, on 100% power (HIGH) for 4 to 5 minutes or till thickened and bubbly, stirring every minute. Stir in tomato (see photo 4). Micro-cook, covered, on 100% power (HIGH) for 1 minute or till hot. Serve over noodles. Serves 4.

1 Thinly slice the meat by holding a sharp knife at a slight angle to the cutting surface. Slice across the grain of the meat, making thin slices 2 to 3 inches long.

The meat is easier to slice when it's partially frozen. Allow 45 to 60 minutes for the meat to partially freeze.

2 During the cooking time, stir the meat two or three times. Use a folding motion to move the pieces of food on the outside of the dish to the center and the pieces of food in the center of the dish to the outside. This helps ensure even cooking.

3 To grate gingerroot, hold a piece of unpeeled gingerroot at a 45-degree angle. Rub it across a fine grating surface, as shown. Or, use a ginger grater like the one on the cutting board. Wrap the unused gingerroot in a paper towel and refrigerate.

4 Gently stir in the tomato wedges. These are stirred in at the last minute so they just heat through, but don't lose their shape.

Hot Turkey Salad

¾ **pound boneless turkey fillets *or* steaks**
3 **tablespoons cold water**
3 **tablespoons tarragon vinegar**
2 **tablespoons chopped onion**
1 **tablespoon sugar**
1 **teaspoon cornstarch**
½ **teaspoon salt**
¼ **teaspoon dry mustard**
¼ **teaspoon celery seed**
   Dash pepper
3 **cups torn fresh spinach**
2 **cups shredded cabbage**
½ **cup sliced radishes**
2 **hard-cooked eggs, sliced**

154 calories per serving

With a sharp knife slice turkey into bite-size strips. Place turkey in a 3-quart nonmetal casserole. Micro-cook turkey, covered, on 100% power (HIGH) for 3 to 4 minutes or till turkey is almost done, stirring two or three times (see photo 2, page 60). Remove turkey from the casserole and drain well.

For dressing, in the same casserole combine water, vinegar, onion, sugar, cornstarch, salt, mustard, celery seed, and pepper. Micro-cook, uncovered, on 100% power (HIGH) for 2 minutes or till mixture is thickened and bubbly, stirring every 30 seconds.

Return turkey to casserole. Add spinach, cabbage, and radishes. Toss to coat with hot dressing. Micro-cook, uncovered, on 100% power (HIGH) for 2 minutes or till heated through, stirring once. Carefully fold in eggs. Serves 4.

Quick Beef Stew

4 **beef cubed steaks (1 pound)**
1 **10¾-ounce can condensed tomato soup**
½ **cup water**
1 **medium onion, cut into 8 wedges**
1 **teaspoon instant beef bouillon granules**
1 **teaspoon dried savory, crushed**
⅛ **teaspoon garlic powder**
⅛ **teaspoon pepper**
1¼ **cups sliced zucchini**
1 **8¾-ounce can whole kernel corn, drained**

249 calories per serving

With a sharp knife slice steaks into bite-size strips. Place meat in a 2-quart nonmetal casserole. Micro-cook meat, covered, on 100% power (HIGH) for 3 to 4 minutes or till meat is no longer pink, stirring two or three times (see photo 2, page 60). Drain.

Stir in soup, water, onion, bouillon granules, savory, garlic powder, and pepper, then add zucchini and corn. Micro-cook, covered, on 100% power (HIGH) for 13 minutes more or till zucchini is tender. Ladle mixture into soup bowls. Makes 4 servings.

Attention, Microwave Owners!

Recipes with microwave directions were tested in countertop microwave ovens that operate on 600 to 700 watts. Times are approximate because microwave ovens vary by manufacturer.

Pork Strips in Pineapple Sauce

1 pound lean boneless pork
1 clove garlic, minced
1 9-ounce package frozen Italian green beans
1 cup frozen crinkle-cut carrots
1 8-ounce can pineapple tidbits (juice pack)
1 tablespoon cornstarch
½ teaspoon instant beef bouillon granules
⅛ teaspoon ground cinnamon

245 calories per serving

Trim separable fat from meat (see photo 1, page 24). Partially freeze meat. Thinly slice meat across the grain into bite-size strips (see photo 1, page 60). Place meat and garlic in a 2-quart nonmetal casserole. Micro-cook meat mixture, covered, on 100% power (HIGH) for 5 minutes or till meat is no longer pink, stirring two or three times (see photo 2, page 60).

Add beans and carrots to the meat mixture. Micro-cook, covered, on 100% power (HIGH) 7 to 9 minutes more or till pork is cooked and vegetables are tender, stirring three or four times. Drain off cooking liquid and reserve.

Drain pineapple, reserving juice. Add enough of the cooking liquid to reserved pineapple juice to measure ¾ cup of liquid. In a 2-cup measure combine pineapple juice mixture, cornstarch, bouillon granules, and cinnamon. Micro-cook, uncovered, on 100% power (HIGH) for 2 to 3 minutes or till thickened and bubbly, stirring every 30 seconds.

Stir pineapple and pineapple juice mixture into meat mixture and mix well. Micro-cook, uncovered, on 100% power (HIGH) for 1 to 2 minutes or till heated through. Makes 4 servings.

Easy Chop Suey

Make this dish even easier by substituting 2 cups of warmed chow mein noodles for the rice.

¾ pound lean boneless pork
1 cup sliced celery
3 green onions, bias-sliced into 1-inch pieces
¾ cup cold water
4 teaspoons cornstarch
1 tablespoon soy sauce
1 teaspoon instant chicken bouillon granules
1 16-ounce can bean sprouts, drained, *or* 2 cups fresh bean sprouts
1 4-ounce can sliced mushrooms, drained
2 tablespoons sliced pimiento
2 cups hot cooked rice

245 calories per serving

Trim separable fat from meat (see photo 1, page 24). Partially freeze meat. Thinly slice meat across the grain into bite-size strips (see photo 1, page 60). Place meat in a 2-quart nonmetal casserole. Micro-cook meat, covered, on 100% power (HIGH) for 4 minutes or until meat is no longer pink, stirring two or three times (see photo 2, page 60).

Add celery and onions to meat. Micro-cook, covered, on 100% power (HIGH) about 4 minutes more or until celery is crisp-tender, stirring twice. In a small bowl stir together water, cornstarch, soy sauce, and bouillon granules. Stir mixture into meat mixture. Micro-cook, uncovered, on 100% power (HIGH) for 4 minutes or till thickened and bubbly, stirring twice.

Stir in sprouts, mushrooms, and pimiento. Micro-cook, uncovered, on 100% power (HIGH) about 2 minutes more or till heated through. Serve over rice. Makes 4 servings.

64

Succulent Baked Poultry

Choosy dieters opt for chicken because it's low in calories but, oh, so flavorful. Cut chicken calories even more by selecting the leaner white pieces such as the breast and wings over the higher-calorie dark pieces. Remove the skin to slash 20 more calories per piece. Then bake till delicately browned and fork tender.

Carrot-Stuffed Chicken Rolls

Carrot-Stuffed Chicken Rolls

2 **whole medium chicken breasts (about 1½ pounds total)**
4 **small carrots**
   Lemon pepper
2 **teaspoons butter *or* margarine**
3 **tablespoons dry white wine**
2 **tablespoons water**
¼ **teaspoon celery salt**
1 **cup thinly sliced celery**
1 **tablespoon cold water**
2 **teaspoons cornstarch**

214 calories per serving

Place one chicken breast on a cutting board, skin side up. Pull skin away from meat, then discard skin. Bone breast and pound halves (see photos 1–2). Repeat with remaining chicken. Cut each carrot into eight sticks (see photo 3). In a medium saucepan cook carrots, covered, in a small amount of boiling water for 5 minutes; drain. Sprinkle chicken lightly with lemon pepper, then dot with butter or margarine. Place eight carrot sticks on each chicken piece and roll chicken around carrots (see photo 4).

Place rolls, seam side down, in an 8x8x2-inch baking dish. In a bowl combine wine, 2 tablespoons water, and celery salt, then pour over chicken. Cover and bake in a 350° oven for 30 to 35 minutes or till tender. Remove chicken and keep warm.

Measure pan juices, then add water to equal ¾ cup liquid. In a saucepan cook celery, covered, in the liquid for 3 minutes or till tender. Combine 1 tablespoon cold water and cornstarch; stir into celery mixture. Cook and stir till thickened and bubbly, then cook and stir 2 minutes more. Serve sauce over chicken. Serves 4.

1 Place the skinned whole chicken breast on a cutting board, meat side up. Starting to one side of the breastbone, use a thin, sharp knife to cut the meat away from the bone. Cut as close to the bone as possible, as shown. Press the flat side of the knife against the rib bones and cut using a sawing motion. Gently pull the meat away from the rib bones as you cut. Repeat on the other side.

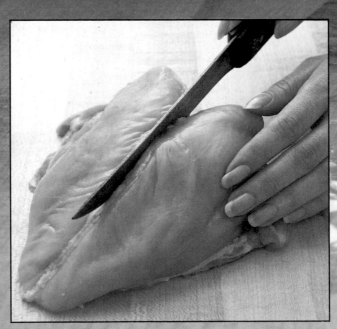

2 Place a chicken breast half between two pieces of clear plastic wrap. Gently pound the chicken with the smooth side of a meat mallet. Work from the center to the edges to form a rectangle ⅛ inch thick.

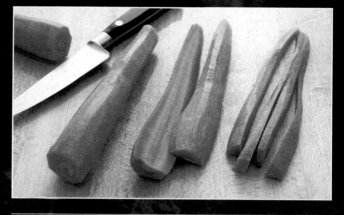

3 With a sharp knife cut each of the carrots in half lengthwise. Cut each in half again to make four carrot sticks. Now cut each carrot stick in half again to make eight short, thin carrot sticks.

4 Place eight of the cooked carrot sticks across the center of each chicken breast. Roll up the chicken jelly-roll style around the carrot sticks. Press the edges of the chicken together with your fingers.

Ham-and-Cheese-Filled Chicken Rolls

The "cheese" comes from bottled blue cheese dressing.

2 whole medium chicken breasts
    (about 1½ pounds total)
3 tablespoons low-calorie blue cheese
    salad dressing
4 thin slices boiled ham (4 ounces)
¼ cup toasted wheat germ
2 tablespoons snipped parsley
1 beaten egg

267 calories per serving

Place one chicken breast on a cutting board, skin side up. Pull the skin away from the meat, then discard skin. Bone breast and pound halves (see photos 1–2, pages 66–67). Repeat with the remaining chicken breast.

Spread each chicken piece with about 2 teaspoons of salad dressing, then add a ham slice. Starting from the short side, fold in sides and roll up jelly-roll style, pressing roll shut (see photo 4, page 67). Repeat with remaining chicken.

In a bowl combine wheat germ and parsley. Dip chicken in beaten egg, then roll in wheat germ and parsley mixture. Place chicken in an 8x8x2-inch baking dish. Bake in a 350° oven for 30 to 35 minutes or till chicken is tender. Serves 4.

Chicken Parmesan

3 whole medium chicken breasts
    (about 2¼ pounds total)
⅓ cup grated Parmesan cheese
¼ teaspoon Italian seasoning,
    crushed
¼ cup sliced green onion
1 tablespoon butter *or* margarine
1 tablespoon all-purpose flour
½ cup skim milk
½ of a 10-ounce package frozen
    chopped spinach, thawed and drained
1 tablespoon chopped pimiento

206 calories per serving

Place one chicken breast on a cutting board, skin side up. Pull the skin away from the meat, then discard skin. Bone chicken breast (see photo 1, page 66). Repeat with remaining breasts.

In a small mixing bowl combine Parmesan cheese and Italian seasoning. Roll chicken pieces in cheese mixture to coat lightly; set remaining cheese mixture aside.

Arrange pieces in an 8x8x2-inch baking dish. In a small saucepan cook onion in hot butter or margarine till tender but not brown. Stir in flour, then add milk all at once. Cook and stir till thickened and bubbly; stir in drained spinach and pimiento. Spoon spinach mixture over chicken and sprinkle with remaining cheese mixture. Bake, uncovered, in a 350° oven for 30 to 35 minutes or till tender. Makes 6 servings.

Curried Pinwheels

Apple, raisins, coconut, curry, and peanuts add zesty Indian flavor.

2 whole medium chicken breasts (about 1½ pounds total)
1 medium apple, cored and finely chopped
¼ cup raisins
2 tablespoons coconut
¾ cup hot water
1 teaspoon curry powder
½ teaspoon instant chicken bouillon granules
1 tablespoon cold water
2 teaspoons cornstarch
1 tablespoon chopped peanuts

225 calories per serving

Place one chicken breast on a cutting board, skin side up. Pull the skin away from the meat, then discard skin. Bone breast and pound halves (see photo 1–2, pages 66–67). Repeat with the remaining chicken breast.

In a small mixing bowl combine apple, raisins, and coconut. Spoon mixture onto chicken breast halves. Starting from a short side, roll up jelly-roll style (see photo 4, page 67). Place chicken, seam side down, in an 8x8x2-inch baking dish. In a small bowl combine hot water, curry powder, and bouillon granules, then pour over chicken.

Bake, covered, in a 350° oven for 30 to 35 minutes or till chicken is tender. Transfer chicken to a serving platter; cover with foil to keep warm. For sauce, strain cooking juices, reserving ½ cup. In a small saucepan combine cold water and cornstarch; add reserved cooking juices. Cook and stir till bubbly, then cook and stir 2 minutes more. To serve, cut each chicken roll into four slices. Serve sauce over slices and sprinkle with peanuts. Makes 4 servings.

Brandied Tarragon Chicken

2 whole medium chicken breasts (about 1½ pounds total)
¼ cup brandy
1 2½-ounce jar sliced mushrooms
1 teaspoon snipped fresh tarragon or ¼ teaspoon dried tarragon, crushed
¼ teaspoon salt
¼ teaspoon pepper
Sprigs of fresh tarragon (optional)

217 calories per serving

Place one chicken breast on a cutting board, skin side up. Pull the skin away from the meat, then discard skin. Bone breast (see photo 1, page 66). Repeat with the remaining chicken breast.

In a small mixing bowl combine brandy, *undrained* mushrooms, tarragon, salt, and pepper. Place chicken pieces in an 8x8x2-inch baking dish. Pour brandy mixture over chicken. Turn pieces to coat.

Bake, covered, in a 350° oven for 30 to 35 minutes or till chicken is tender. Baste with cooking juices once. To serve, transfer chicken and cooking juices to a serving platter. Garnish with tarragon, if desired. Makes 4 servings.

Sensational Roasted Meats

Treat yourself to an elegant roast *and stay* trim. Not possible you say? Sure it is. Here's the proof. Choose lean cuts of meat, remove the excess fat, and watch calories disappear.

Pork Roast Florentine

Pork Roast Florentine

Ask your butcher to loosen the backbone—it makes the roast easier to carve.

1 **3-pound pork loin center rib roast, backbone loosened**
1 **10-ounce package frozen chopped spinach, thawed and well drained**
½ **cup shredded carrot**
1 **small apple, cored and chopped**
½ **teaspoon salt**
¼ **teaspoon dried basil, crushed**
1 **5½-ounce can (about ⅔ cup) apple juice**
1 **tablespoon soy sauce**
2 **teaspoons cornstarch**
¼ **cup shredded carrot**
2 **tablespoons thinly sliced green onion**
   Cherry tomatoes (optional)
   Parsley sprigs (optional)

270 calories per serving

Trim separable fat from meat (see photo 1, page 24). Cut eight pockets in the meaty side of roast (see photo 1). In a medium bowl stir together well-drained spinach, ½ cup carrot, apple, salt, and basil. Spoon a generous ¼ cup of spinach mixture into each pocket (see photo 2).

Place roast, bone side down, in a shallow roasting pan. Insert a meat thermometer into the roast (see photo 3). Roast meat in a 325° oven for 1¾ to 2¼ hours or till thermometer registers 170°. Remove roast from the oven. Let stand 15 minutes.

For sauce, in a small saucepan combine apple juice, soy sauce, and cornstarch. Stir in ¼ cup carrot and onion. Cook and stir till thickened and bubbly, then cook and stir 2 minutes more. Transfer roast to a cutting board. Cut away backbone, removing as little meat as possible (see photo 4). Place roast on a platter. Garnish with tomatoes and parsley, if desired. To serve, place a fork in top of roast to steady meat and cut between pockets. Serve sauce with meat. Serves 8.

1 With a sharp knife, cut eight pockets in the meaty side of the pork loin center rib roast. Position the pockets between the bones, as shown. The pockets should be cut about halfway into the meat of the pork roast.

3 Insert a meat thermometer into the end of the roast so its bulb rests in the center of the thickest part of the meat. It should not rest in the filling or fat, or touch the bone or bottom of the pan. This ensures that the thermometer accurately measures the internal temperature of the meat.

2 Hold the pocket open with one hand and spoon the spinach mixture into the pocket with the other hand, as shown. Notice the shape of the bone in the roast—it makes its own rack. When the rib bones are left on the roast, no rack is needed.

4 To make carving easier, remove the backbone after the roast is cooked. Begin by cutting between the roast and the bone, staying as close to the bone as possible. Then, gently pull the bone away from the roast as you continue cutting, removing as little of the meat as possible.

Roast Eye of Round with Vegetables

Chutney (CHUT-nee) lends a delicate flavor to the meat and gives the roast a moist, glazed appearance.

1 **2-pound beef eye of round roast**
  Salt
  Pepper
3 **tablespoons finely chopped chutney**
1 **16-ounce package frozen French-style green beans**
1 **large onion, cut into wedges**
½ **cup apple juice**
2 **tablespoons chopped pimiento**
1½ **teaspoons cornstarch**
⅛ **teaspoon dried thyme, crushed**

169 calories per serving

Trim separable fat from meat (see photo 1, page 24). Place meat on a rack in a shallow roasting pan. Sprinkle with salt and pepper. Insert a meat thermometer into the roast (see photo 3, page 73). Roast in a 325° oven for 1½ to 2 hours for rare or till thermometer registers 140°. Roast to 160° for medium or to 170° for well-done. Spoon chutney over top of roast, then roast 10 to 15 minutes more. Remove meat from the oven. Let stand 15 minutes.

Meanwhile, for vegetables, in a covered saucepan cook green beans and onion in a small amount of boiling salted water for 4 to 5 minutes or till onion is tender. Drain beans and onions, then set aside. In the same saucepan combine apple juice, pimiento, cornstarch, and thyme. Cook and stir till thickened and bubbly, then cook and stir 2 minutes more. Stir in beans and onion. Carve meat into 16 thin slices. Serve on a platter with vegetables. Makes 8 servings.

Pork with Curry Relish

1 **2-pound boneless pork loin top loin roast**
  Salt
  Pepper
½ **cup cold water**
2 **teaspoons cornstarch**
½ **to 1 teaspoon curry powder**
½ **teaspoon instant chicken bouillon granules**
1 **medium cooking apple, cored and chopped**
2 **tablespoons finely snipped dried apricots**

175 calories per serving

Trim separable fat from meat (see photo 1, page 24). Place meat on a rack in a shallow roasting pan. Sprinkle with salt and pepper. Insert a meat thermometer into the roast (see photo 3, page 73). Roast in a 325° oven for 1 to 1¼ hours or till meat thermometer registers 170°. Remove meat from the oven. Let meat stand 15 minutes.

Meanwhile, for sauce, in a medium saucepan combine water, cornstarch, curry, and bouillon granules. Cook and stir till thickened and bubbly. Stir in apple and apricots. Cover and simmer for 2 to 3 minutes or till apple is tender, stirring occasionally. Carve meat into eight slices. Serve sauce over meat. Makes 8 servings.

Roast Beef with Mushroom Sauce

A delicate wine flavor rounds out this mushroom sauce, so that no one will suspect you're counting calories.

1 **3-pound beef top round roast**
½ **teaspoon salt**
½ **teaspoon dried marjoram, crushed**
¼ **teaspoon pepper**
1 **14½-ounce can beef broth**
4 **teaspoons cornstarch**
1 **4-ounce can sliced mushrooms, drained**
¼ **cup dry red wine**
⅛ **teaspoon dried marjoram, crushed**

163 calories per serving

Trim separable fat from meat (see photo 1, page 24). Place meat on a rack in a shallow roasting pan. In a small bowl combine salt, ½ teaspoon marjoram, and pepper, then rub over meat. Insert a meat thermometer into the roast (see photo 3, page 73). Roast in a 325° oven for 1½ to 2 hours for medium-rare or till meat thermometer registers 150°. Roast to 160° for medium or to 170° for well-done. Remove meat from the oven. Let stand 15 minutes.

Meanwhile, for sauce, in a small saucepan combine beef broth and cornstarch. Cook and stir till thickened and bubbly, then cook and stir 2 minutes more. Stir in mushrooms, red wine, and ⅛ teaspoon marjoram. Heat through. Carve roast by bias-slicing across the grain into 10 slices. Serve sauce with meat. Makes 10 servings.

Veal à l'Orange

Cardamom, a distinctive spice belonging to the ginger family, subtly flavors the orange sauce.

1 **3-pound veal leg sirloin roast**
1 **cup orange juice**
1 **tablespoon cornstarch**
¼ **teaspoon chicken bouillon granules**
¼ **teaspoon ground cardamom**
1 **11-ounce can mandarin orange sections, drained**
1 **tablespoon orange liqueur (optional)**

182 calories per serving

Trim separable fat from meat (see photo 1, page 24). Place meat on a rack in a shallow roasting pan. Insert a meat thermometer into the roast (see photo 3, page 73). Roast in a 325° oven for 1¾ to 2 hours or till thermometer registers 170°. Remove meat from the oven. Let stand 15 minutes.

Meanwhile, for orange sauce, in a small saucepan combine orange juice, cornstarch, bouillon granules, and cardamom. Cook and stir till thickened and bubbly, then cook and stir 2 minutes more. Add orange sections and orange liqueur, if desired. Heat through. Carve meat into 10 slices. Serve with orange sauce. Serves 10.

Spirited Marinades

Make your main dishes say delectable, not diet, with marinades. By soaking meats in flavorful mixtures of herbs, spices, and wine or vinegar you can give them lots of flavor with few calories. What's more, you can often recycle the marinade as a sauce.

Sherry-Marinated Steaks

Sherry-Marinated Steaks

1   **pound beef top round steak,**
      cut ¾ inch thick
¼   **cup sliced green onion**
1   **clove garlic, minced**
½   **cup dry sherry**
1   **2½-ounce jar sliced**
      mushrooms, drained
1   **tablespoon snipped parsley**
      (see photo 4)
2   **teaspoons cornstarch**
¼   **teaspoon instant beef bouillon granules**
    Green onions (optional)
    Tomato wedges (optional)

164 calories per serving

Trim separable fat from meat (see photo 1, page 24). Cut into four pieces and place in a plastic bag (see photo 1). Set bag in a deep bowl. Add sliced onion, garlic, and ¼ teaspoon *pepper*, then pour sherry over mixture (see photo 2). Close bag tightly and turn to coat meat. Marinate in the refrigerator for 8 to 24 hours, turning bag once or twice (see photo 3).

Drain steaks well, reserving marinade. Place on an unheated rack in a broiler pan. Broil 3 inches from the heat for 5 minutes (see photo 2, page 48). Turn steaks with tongs and broil 5 to 6 minutes more or till desired doneness.

Meanwhile, for sauce, add enough water to reserved marinade to measure 1 cup liquid. In a small saucepan combine marinade mixture, mushrooms, parsley, cornstarch, and bouillon granules. Cook and stir till thickened and bubbly, then cook and stir 2 minutes more. Place steaks on a hot platter (see photo 5). Spoon sauce over steaks. Garnish with whole green onions and tomato wedges, if desired. Serves 4.

1 Place the meat in a large plastic bag. Putting everything into one plastic bag makes it easier to distribute the marinade and simplifies cleanup.

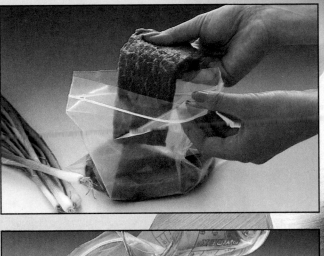

2 Pour the marinade mixture into the plastic bag, as shown. Place the plastic bag inside a deep bowl to prevent any accidental leakage and to make transporting the bag easier. Close the bag securely and turn it over a few times to coat all of the meat with the marinade mixture.

3 Remember to turn the plastic bag over occasionally during the marinating time, so that the marinade is evenly distributed over all the surfaces of the meat.

4 Place a couple of sprigs of fresh parsley in a custard cup or measuring cup. Snip with kitchen shears. One or two sprigs will yield about 1 tablespoon of snipped parsley.

5 Keep the marinated steaks hot and juicy by serving them on a heated sizzle platter.

Fancy Fish Fillets

1 pound fresh *or* frozen sole *or* flounder
   fillets
¼ cup water
¼ cup dry white wine
½ teaspoon dried basil, crushed
½ teaspoon instant chicken bouillon
   granules
   Nonstick spray coating
1 8-ounce package frozen brussels sprouts
¾ cup plain low-fat yogurt
4 teaspoons cornstarch
1 tablespoon chopped pimiento

147 calories per serving

Thaw fish, if frozen. Separate into fillets. Place fish in a plastic bag (see photo 1, page 78). Set bag in a deep bowl. For marinade, in a small bowl combine water, wine, basil, and bouillon granules. Pour marinade over fish in bag (see photo 2, page 78). Close bag tightly and turn bag to coat fish. Marinate for 1 hour at room temperature or 6 hours in the refrigerator, turning bag once or twice (see photo 3, page 78).

Drain fillets well, reserving the marinade. Spray a 12x7½x2-inch baking dish with nonstick coating. Place fillets in baking dish. Bake, uncovered, in a 450° oven till fish flakes easily with a fork (see photo 3, page 85). Allow 5 to 6 minutes for each ½-inch thickness.

Meanwhile for sauce, in a medium saucepan cook brussels sprouts according to package directions. Drain well. When cool enough to handle, cut brussels sprouts in half. In the same saucepan combine yogurt and cornstarch. Stir in reserved marinade and pimiento. Cook and stir till thickened and bubbly, then cook and stir 2 minutes more. Stir in brussels sprouts and heat through. Transfer fish to a serving platter. Spoon sauce over the fish. Makes 4 servings.

Harvest Pork Chops

Apple rings, cider, and pork chops—yum!

4 pork chops, cut ½ inch thick
   (about 1⅓ pounds)
½ cup apple juice *or* apple cider
1 tablespoon snipped chives
1 clove garlic, minced
¼ teaspoon dried basil, crushed
¼ teaspoon dried oregano, crushed
   Salt
   Pepper
4 thinly sliced apple rings

182 calories per serving

Trim separable fat from chops (see photo 1, page 24). Place chops in a plastic bag (see photo 1, page 78). Set bag in a deep bowl. For marinade, in a small bowl combine apple juice, chives, garlic, basil, and oregano. Pour over meat in bag (see photo 2, page 78). Close bag tightly and turn bag to coat meat. Marinate in the refrigerator for 8 to 24 hours, turning bag once or twice (see photo 3, page 78).

Drain chops well and place on an unheated rack in a broiler pan. Broil chops 3 to 4 inches from the heat for 6 minutes (see photo 2, page 48). Turn chops and broil 6 minutes more. Sprinkle with salt and pepper. Place an apple ring on top of each chop. Broil 2 minutes more. Serves 4.

Lemon-Marinated Steak

1 pound beef top round steak,
   cut ¾ inch thick
½ teaspoon finely shredded lemon peel
3 tablespoons lemon juice
3 tablespoons water
1 tablespoon cooking oil
1 tablespoon sliced green onion
1 teaspoon Worcestershire sauce
½ teaspoon instant beef bouillon granules
⅛ teaspoon pepper
   Snipped parsley (optional)

157 calories per serving

Trim separable fat from meat (see photo 1, page 24). Pierce all surfaces of meat with a long-tined fork. Place meat in a plastic bag (see photo 1, page 78). Set bag in a deep bowl.

For marinade, in a small bowl combine lemon peel, lemon juice, water, oil, onion, Worcestershire sauce, bouillon granules, and pepper. Pour over meat in bag (see photo 2, page 78). Close bag tightly and turn to coat meat. Marinate in the refrigerator for 8 to 24 hours, turning bag once or twice (see photo 3, page 78).

Drain meat well, reserving marinade. Place meat on a rack in an unheated broiler pan. Broil meat 4 inches from heat for 5 minutes (see photo 2, page 48). Brush meat with marinade and turn with tongs. Broil for 5 to 7 minutes more or till desired doneness, brushing with marinade occasionally. Transfer meat to a serving platter and carve across the grain into thin slices. Garnish with parsley, if desired. Makes 4 servings.

Pineapple-Sauced Fish

1 pound fresh *or* frozen haddock fillets
½ cup unsweetened pineapple juice
1 teaspoon minced dried onion
¼ teaspoon salt
⅛ teaspoon dried mint, crushed
   Nonstick spray coating
1 teaspoon cornstarch
2 tablespoons snipped parsley
   (see photo 4, page 79)
   Mint sprigs (optional)

112 calories per serving

Thaw fish, if frozen. Separate into fillets. Place fish in a plastic bag (see photo 1, page 78). Set bag in a deep bowl. For marinade, in a small bowl combine pineapple juice, onion, salt, and mint. Pour over fish in bag (see photo 2, page 78). Close bag tightly and turn bag to coat fish. Marinate for 1 hour at room temperature or 6 hours in the refrigerator, turning once or twice.

Drain fish well, reserving the marinade. Spray a 12x7x2-inch baking dish with nonstick coating. Place fish in baking dish. (If fillets vary in thickness, turn under any thin portions.) Bake, uncovered, in a 450° oven till fish flakes easily with a fork (see photo 3, page 85). Allow 5 to 6 minutes for each ½-inch thickness.

Meanwhile, for sauce, in a small saucepan combine reserved marinade and cornstarch. Cook and stir till thickened and bubbly, then cook and stir 2 minutes more. Transfer fish to a serving platter and serve with sauce. Sprinkle with parsley. Garnish with mint, if desired. Serves 4.

Delicious Steamed Fish

Try steam heat! It's perfect for cooking fish. Not only does steaming keep the fish moist, it also helps the fish retain its shape and delicate texture. Because steam heat relies on water rather than heavy fats or oil, it makes for great low-calorie eating—naturally.

Spicy Steamed Fish

Spicy Steamed Fish

For a quick reference to other delicious fish selections, refer to the tip box on page 87.

1 **pound fresh *or* frozen halibut steaks *or* other lean fish steaks *or* fillets**
1 **5½-ounce can hot-style tomato juice *or* one 6-ounce can spicy vegetable juice cocktail**
1 **medium tomato, peeled, seeded, and chopped (½ cup)**
2 **tablespoons chopped onion**
2 **tablespoons chopped green pepper**
1 **teaspoon lemon juice**
   Fresh dill (optional)

196 calories per serving

Thaw fish, if frozen. For sauce, in a small saucepan combine tomato juice or vegetable juice cocktail, tomato, onion, green pepper, and lemon juice. Bring to boiling; reduce heat. Simmer, uncovered, about 12 minutes or till sauce thickens and is reduced to 1 cup.

Meanwhile, place a wire rack in a 10-inch skillet with a tight-fitting lid. Add water until it almost reaches the rack (see photo 1). Bring water to boiling. Place fish on the rack (see photo 2). Cover the pan and steam 6 to 8 minutes for steaks, 4 to 6 minutes per ½ inch of thickness for fillets, or till fish flakes easily with a fork (see photo 3).

Carefully transfer fish from the rack to a serving platter (see photo 4). Pour sauce over fish. Garnish with dill, if desired. Makes 4 servings.

1 Pour water into a 10-inch skillet till it almost reaches the rack, as shown. If there's not enough water in the skillet, all of it may boil away, scorching the pan. If there's too much water, the fish boils rather than steams and some of the fish flavor is lost in the steaming liquid.

2 Bring the water in the skillet to boiling, then carefully arrange the fish steaks or fillets on the rack with tongs or a spatula, as shown. Don't use your hands to arrange the fish because the heat from the steam may burn them.

Test for doneness

3 Insert the fork tines into the fish at a 45-degree angle. Then, twist the fork gently. If the fish resists flaking and is still translucent, it's underdone.

The fish is done when it is opaque and flakes easily.

The fish is overdone if it looks dry or mealy and falls apart easily.

Underdone

Done

Overdone

4 Slide the spatula completely underneath each fish steak or fillet. This helps to keep the fish from breaking apart as you lift it. If you run the spatula parallel to the rungs of the rack, as shown, it is easier to get under the piece of fish than trying to go across the rungs.

Now, carefully transfer each piece of fish to a serving platter.

Steamed Salmon with Horseradish Sauce

Just enough horseradish to tingle your taste buds.

  2   **small fresh** *or* **frozen salmon steaks (½ pound)**
  ½   **cup skim milk**
  1   **tablespoon snipped chives** *or* **green onion tops**
1½   **teaspoons cornstarch**
  ⅛   **teaspoon salt**
  2   **teaspoons prepared horseradish**
  ½   **teaspoon lemon juice**
      Alfalfa sprouts (optional)
      Lemon wedges (optional)

208 calories per serving

Thaw fish, if frozen. Place a wire rack in a 10-inch skillet with a tight-fitting lid. Add water until it almost reaches rack (see photo 1, page 84). Bring water to boiling. Place steaks on rack (see photo 2, page 84). Cover pan and steam 6 to 8 minutes or till fish flakes easily with a fork (see photo 3, page 85).

Meanwhile, for sauce, in a small saucepan combine milk, chives or onion tops, cornstarch, and salt. Cook and stir till thickened and bubbly, cook and stir 2 minutes more. Remove from heat, then stir in horseradish and lemon juice. Carefully transfer fish to a serving platter (see photo 4, page 85). Pour sauce atop. Garnish with alfalfa sprouts and lemon wedges, if desired. Makes 2 servings.

Microwave Directions: (See tip box, page 62). Place fish in an 8x8x2-inch nonmetal baking dish. Cover with vented plastic wrap. In a countertop microwave oven on 100% power (HIGH) cook for 3½ to 4 minutes or till fish flakes easily with a fork (see photo 3, page 85). In a small nonmetal bowl combine milk, chives, cornstarch, and salt. Micro-cook, uncovered, on 100% power (HIGH) for 1½ to 2½ minutes or till thickened and bubbly, stirring every 30 seconds. Stir in horseradish and lemon juice. Continue as above.

Steamed Snapper and Squash

  ½   **pound fresh** *or* **frozen red snapper fillets** *or* **other lean fish fillets (2 fillets)**
  4   **ounces yellow summer squash** *or* **zucchini**
  3   **ounces fresh** *or* **frozen pea pods**
  ½   **cup cold water**
1½   **teaspoons cornstarch**
  ¾   **teaspoon instant chicken bouillon granules**
  ¼   **teaspoon dried thyme, crushed**
  1   **tablespoon butter** *or* **margarine**
  ⅔   **cup hot cooked rice**

250 calories per serving

Thaw fish, if frozen. Remove and discard skin, if present. Slice squash diagonally into ¼-inch-thick pieces. Clean fresh pea pods and remove strings, if necessary (see photo 4, page 37). (*Or,* run warm water over frozen pea pods to thaw.)

Place a wire rack in a 10-inch skillet with a tight-fitting lid. Add water until it almost reaches the rack (see photo 1, page 84). Bring to boiling. Place fish, sliced squash, and pea pods on rack (see photo 2, page 84). Cover pan and steam for 4 to 6 minutes per ½ inch thickness of fillets or till fish flakes easily with a fork and vegetables are crisp-tender (see photo 3, page 85).

Meanwhile, for sauce, in a small saucepan combine cold water, cornstarch, bouillon granules, and thyme. Cook and stir till thickened and bubbly, then cook and stir 2 minutes more. Stir in the butter or margarine till melted.

Carefully transfer fish and vegetables from the rack to a serving platter (see photo 4, page 85). Serve sauce over fish, vegetables, and hot cooked rice. Makes 2 servings.

Vegetable-Sauced Fish Fillets

1	16-ounce package frozen fish fillets
1	medium carrot, cut into thin slices
1	stalk celery, cut into thin slices
1	cup skim milk
1	tablespoon cornstarch
¼	teaspoon salt
¼	teaspoon dried dillweed

201 calories per serving

Thaw fish at room temperature for 20 to 30 minutes. Cut into four portions. Place a rack in a 10-inch skillet with a tight-fitting lid. Add water until it almost reaches rack (see photo 1, page 84). Bring water to boiling. Place fish on rack (see photo 2, page 84). Cover pan and steam 12 to 14 minutes or till fish flakes easily with a fork (see photo 3, page 85).

Meanwhile, for sauce, in a small saucepan cook carrot and celery in a small amount of boiling salted water about 5 minutes or till crisp-tender; drain. In the same saucepan combine milk, cornstarch, salt, and dillweed. Cook and stir till thickened and bubbly, then cook and stir 2 minutes more. Add vegetables and heat through.

Carefully transfer fish from the rack to a serving platter (see photo 4, page 85). Serve sauce over fish. Makes 4 servings.

Crab with Lime Sauce

2	pounds frozen cooked king crab legs
½	cup cold water
¾	teaspoon instant chicken bouillon granules
½	teaspoon cornstarch
2	tablespoons butter *or* margarine
5	teaspoons lime juice

195 calories per serving

Thaw crab. Cut into four pieces. Place a wire rack in a 10-inch skillet with a tight-fitting lid. Add water until it almost reaches rack (see photo 1, page 84). Bring water to boiling. Place crab on rack over boiling water (see photo 2, page 84). Cover and steam for 5 minutes or till hot.

For sauce, in a small saucepan combine cold water, bouillon granules, and cornstarch. Cook and stir till thickened and bubbly, then cook and stir 2 minutes more. Add butter or margarine and lime juice. Stir till butter or margarine is melted. Use as a dip for crab. Serves 4.

Figuring Out Fish

All fish are not created equal! Although most fish are leaner than many types of meat and poultry, some fish are leaner than others. The leanest fish (with less than 5 percent fat) include catfish, cod, perch, flounder, sole, haddock, smelt, whiting, and red snapper. "Fat" fish include lake trout, eel, mackerel, tuna, salmon, swordfish, and whitefish. If you must severely limit your fat intake, depend on the first group. If not, both are deliciously low-calorie.

Sizzling Stir-Frys

Stir up excitement at mealtime. Try your hand at stir-frying. As the name implies, this cooking method uses a constant stirring motion to quickly cook foods. That means you need very little fat or oil. The results are low-calorie and delicious.

Garlic Chicken

Garlic Chicken

2 whole large chicken breasts (2 pounds total), skinned and boned (see photo 1, page 66)
3 cups fresh pea pods *or* **two 6-ounce packages frozen pea pods**
3 large carrots
4 green onions
5 cloves garlic
⅓ cup cold water
3 tablespoons soy sauce
2 tablespoons dry sherry
1 tablespoon cornstarch
2 tablespoons cooking oil

300 calories per serving

Cut chicken into 1-inch pieces. Clean fresh pea pods and remove strings, if necessary (see photo 4, page 37). Or, run warm water over the frozen pea pods to partially thaw. Bias-slice carrots and thinly slice onions (see photo 1). Mince garlic (see photos 2–3). Set aside.

In a small bowl combine cold water, soy sauce, sherry, and cornstarch. Set aside.

Preheat a wok or large skillet over high heat; add *half* of the cooking oil. Add carrots and garlic. Using a spatula or long-handled spoon, gently lift and turn the food with a folding motion. Keep food moving at all times or it will burn (see photo 4). Stir-fry for 3 minutes. Add pea pods and onions. Stir-fry for 2 minutes more or till vegetables are crisp-tender. Transfer vegetables to a bowl.

Add remaining cooking oil to the hot wok or skillet. Add *half* of the chicken, then stir-fry about 3 minutes (see photo 5). Remove chicken. Stir-fry remaining chicken about 3 minutes. Return all chicken to the wok or skillet. Push chicken from the center of the wok. Stir cornstarch mixture and add to the center of the wok or skillet. Cook and stir till thickened and bubbly, then cook and stir 1 minute more (see photo 6). Stir vegetables into chicken mixture and cover. Cook 1 minute more. Makes 5 servings.

1 Bias-slice carrots by holding a sharp knife at a 45-degree angle to the cutting board. Cut each carrot into thin slices (about ⅛ inch thick), as shown. These thin slices will cook quickly in the wok as well as give an attractive appearance to the finished dish. The green onions, along with some of their green tops, are cut into thin slices, as shown at the top of the cutting board.

2 Working on a cutting board, crush garlic by holding a wide-blade knife over a clove. Lightly pound the knife with your fist, moving the knife forward to loosen the peel. If you own a garlic press, you'll find it a handy way to mince garlic, too.

3 Remove the thin peel from the garlic and discard it. Cut the garlic into very tiny pieces with a sharp knife, as shown.

4 Use a wide spatula or long-handled spoon to stir-fry. Gently lift and turn the food with a folding motion. Keep the food moving so that it cooks evenly without burning.

6 Push the chicken from the center of the wok. Stir the cornstarch mixture and pour it into the center of the wok. Cook and stir the mixture till thickened and bubbly, as shown.

5 Stir-fry the chicken with the same folding motion, making sure all sides are cooked. You'll know when the chicken is done by the change in color from pink to beige.

Pork and Zucchini Stir-Fry

1 pound lean boneless pork
2 carrots, thinly bias sliced
   (see photo 1, page 90)
¼ cup cold water
2 tablespoons soy sauce
1 tablespoon cornstarch
1 teaspoon sugar
½ teaspoon instant chicken bouillon
   granules
   Nonstick spray coating
2 small zucchini, cut into julienne strips
1 tablespoon cooking oil
1 cup sliced fresh mushrooms

234 calories per serving

Trim separable fat from meat (see photo 1, page 24). Partially freeze meat. With a sharp knife thinly slice meat across the grain into bite-size strips (see photo 1, page 60). In a medium saucepan cook carrots in boiling water for 2 to 3 minutes or till crisp-tender; drain. In a small bowl stir together cold water, soy sauce, cornstarch, sugar, and bouillon granules. Set aside.

Spray a wok or skillet with nonstick coating. Preheat the wok or skillet over high heat. *(See stir-frying photos 4–6, page 91.)* Add zucchini and stir-fry for 2 to 3 minutes or till crisp-tender; remove from wok or skillet. Add cooking oil to the wok or skillet. Add *half* of meat. Stir-fry for 2 to 3 minutes or till no longer pink. Remove meat from wok or skillet. Stir-fry remaining pork for 2 to 3 minutes or till no longer pink. Return all of the meat to the wok or skillet. Push meat from center of the wok or skillet. Stir cornstarch mixture, then add to center of wok or skillet. Cook and stir till thickened and bubbly. Stir in carrots, zucchini, and mushrooms and cover. Cook 1 to 2 minutes more. Serves 4.

Orange-Beef Stir-Fry

¾ pound beef top round steak
3 cups broccoli, cut into 1-inch pieces
½ teaspoon finely shredded orange peel
½ cup orange juice
2 tablespoons soy sauce
2 teaspoons cornstarch
2 medium oranges
   Nonstick spray coating

183 calories per serving

Trim separable fat from meat (see photo 1, page 24). Partially freeze meat. With a sharp knife thinly slice meat across the grain into bite-size strips (see photo 1, page 60). In a medium saucepan cook broccoli, covered, in a small amount of boiling water about 5 minutes or till crisp-tender; drain. Set aside. In a small bowl stir together orange peel, orange juice, soy sauce, and cornstarch. Set aside.

Working over a bowl, peel and section oranges. First, cut off the peel and white membrane. Then, remove the sections by cutting into the center of the fruit between one section and the membrane. Turn the knife and slide it down the other side of the section next to the membrane. Remove any seeds.

Spray the wok or large skillet with nonstick coating. Preheat the wok or skillet over high heat. *(See stir-frying photos 4–6, page 91.)* Stir-fry meat for 2 to 3 minutes or till brown. Push meat from center of wok or skillet. Stir cornstarch mixture, then add to center of wok or skillet. Cook and stir till thickened and bubbly. Stir in broccoli and orange sections and cover. Cook 1 minute more. Makes 4 servings.

Sesame Veal

1 pound boneless veal *or* lean pork
½ cup water
2 tablespoons sake *or* dry sherry
1 tablespoon cornstarch
1 teaspoon instant chicken bouillon
   granules
¼ teaspoon ground ginger *or*
   ½ teaspoon grated gingerroot
2 tablespoons cooking oil
2 cups fresh asparagus, cut into 1-inch
   pieces *or* one 9-ounce package
   frozen cut asparagus, thawed
4 green onions, bias-sliced into ¼-inch
   pieces
2 medium tomatoes, seeded and
   cut into thin wedges
1 tablespoon sesame seeds, toasted

289 calories per serving

Trim separable fat from meat (see photo 1, page 24). Partially freeze meat. With a sharp knife thinly slice meat across the grain into bite-size strips (see photo 1, page 60). In a bowl combine water, sake or sherry, cornstarch, bouillon granules, and ginger. Set aside.

Preheat a wok or large skillet over high heat; add *half* of the cooking oil. *(See stir-frying photos 4–6, page 91.)* Stir-fry asparagus and onions for 1 minute. Remove from the wok.

Add remaining oil to the wok or skillet. Add *half* of the veal or pork, then stir-fry for 2 minutes. Remove meat. Stir-fry remaining meat for 2 minutes. Return all meat to wok or skillet. Push meat from the center of the wok or skillet. Stir cornstarch mixture, then add to the center of the wok or skillet. Cook and stir till thickened and bubbly. Return vegetables to wok or skillet. Cook and stir 1 minute. Add tomato wedges and cover. Cook 1 minute more. Sprinkle with sesame seeds. Makes 4 servings.

Shrimp and Spinach Stir-Fry

Thaw frozen shrimp by running cold water over them.

¾ pound fresh *or* frozen shrimp in shells
½ cup unsweetened pineapple juice
2 teaspoons cornstarch
2 tablespoons cooking oil
6 cups torn fresh spinach
12 cherry tomatoes, halved

174 calories per serving

Thaw shrimp, if frozen. Shell and devein shrimp (see tip box, below). Halve shrimp lengthwise. In a bowl stir together pineapple juice, cornstarch, and dash *pepper*. Set aside.

Preheat a wok or skillet over high heat; add oil. *(See stir-frying photos 4–6, page 91.)* Stir-fry shrimp for 2 to 3 minutes. Push shrimp from the center of wok or skillet. Stir cornstarch mixture, then add to center of the wok. Cook and stir till thickened and bubbly, then cook and stir 1 minute more. Stir in spinach and tomatoes and cover. Cook 1 minute more. Serves 4.

Shelling Shrimp

To shell shrimp, peel off the legs. Then, hold each shrimp in one hand and peel back the shell with the other hand. Now, cut the body portion of the shell off, leaving the tail shell in place. Or, gently pull on the tail and remove the tail and shell. Leave the tail on when you're making shrimp cocktail or any food eaten by hand. Finally, make a slit along the back of each shrimp and use the tip of a knife to scrape out the black vein. Rinse the shrimp.

Outstanding Omelets

An egg is an egg is an egg—except when it's an omelet! Turn this traditional breakfast favorite into a low-calorie anytime meal. Our fluffy, delicate omelets are stuffed with an assortment of calorie-trimmed fillings and are cooked with the barest minimum of cooking oil. Turn the pages and find exquisite omelets, sure to satisfy even the most discriminating palate.

Asparagus-Cheese Omelet

Asparagus-Cheese Omelets

In season, use ½ pound fresh asparagus in place of the frozen, but precook it for 10 to 15 minutes.

1 **10-ounce package frozen asparagus** *or* **broccoli spears**
1 **cup sliced fresh mushrooms**
¾ **cup skim milk**
2 **teaspoons cornstarch**
2 **tablespoons shredded cheddar cheese** *or* **crumbled blue cheese**
8 **eggs**
¼ **cup water**
½ **teaspoon salt**
⅛ **teaspoon pepper**
   Nonstick spray coating
1½ **teaspoons cooking oil**
   Snipped parsley (optional)

235 calories per serving

For filling, in a medium saucepan cook asparagus or broccoli spears and mushrooms in ½ cup boiling salted water for 5 minutes or till crisp-tender. Drain well, then keep warm.

For sauce, in a small saucepan combine milk, cornstarch, and dash *salt*. Cook and stir till thickened and bubbly, then cook and stir 2 minutes more. Stir in cheddar or blue cheese till it is melted. Keep warm over low heat.

To make omelets, in a bowl beat together eggs, water, ½ teaspoon salt, and pepper till combined but not frothy (see photo 1). Spray a 6- or 8-inch skillet with nonstick coating, then heat the skillet. Add *one-fourth* of the egg mixture, about ½ cup (see photo 2). Cook eggs over medium heat. As eggs set, run a spatula around edge of the skillet, lifting eggs to allow uncooked portion to flow underneath (see photo 3). When eggs are set but still shiny, remove from the heat. Fill omelet with *one-fourth* of the filling and transfer to a warm serving plate (see photos 4–5). Cover with foil to keep warm.

To make *each* of the three remaining omelets, add *½ teaspoon* oil to the hot skillet. Spread oil evenly by tilting and rotating the skillet. Cook and fill as above. Serve sauce with omelets. Sprinkle with parsley, if desired. Serves 4.

1 Beat together the eggs, water, salt, and pepper with a wire whisk or fork till they're combined but not frothy. Overbeating incorporates too much air into the eggs and gives you a rubbery omelet.

2 Start by pouring *one-fourth* of the egg mixture into the heated skillet, as shown. Using a skillet with flared sides makes it easier to remove the omelet, but a straight-sided skillet will work.

3 As the eggs set, run a spatula around the edge of the skillet, lifting the cooked eggs to allow the uncooked portion to flow underneath, as shown. Tipping the pan slightly helps.

Do not let the skillet become too hot or the eggs will be overcooked and tough. Medium heat works best.

4 Arrange or spoon some of the filling across the center of the omelet. Using a spatula, carefully lift one-third of the omelet over the filling, as shown. Repeat with the remaining one-third.

5 Slide the omelet to the side of the skillet. Tilt the skillet and slide the omelet out onto a warm plate, as shown. Cover with foil to keep the omelet warm while preparing the other omelets.

Southwestern Omelets

1 medium tomato, peeled, seeded, and chopped
⅓ cup green chili peppers, rinsed, seeded, and chopped
2 tablespoons sliced green onion
1 tablespoon snipped cilantro *or* parsley
1 small clove garlic, minced
   Dash salt
   Dash ground red pepper
4 eggs
2 tablespoons water
¼ teaspoon salt
   Dash pepper
   Nonstick spray coating
½ teaspoon cooking oil
¼ cup shredded Monterey Jack cheese *or* Monterey Jack cheese with jalapeño peppers (1 ounce)

259 calories per serving

For filling, in a small saucepan mix tomato, chili peppers, onion, cilantro or parsley, garlic, dash salt, and red pepper. Simmer about 3 minutes or till heated through; stir often. Keep warm.

(See omelet-making photos 1–5, pages 96–97.) To make omelets, in a bowl beat together eggs, water, ¼ teaspoon salt, and pepper till combined but not frothy. Spray a 6- or 8-inch skillet with nonstick coating, then heat the skillet. Add *half* of the egg mixture, about ½ cup, then cook over medium heat. As eggs set, run a spatula around *edge* of the skillet, lifting the eggs to allow uncooked portion to flow underneath. When eggs are set but still shiny, remove from the heat. Fill each omelet with *half* of the filling and transfer to a warm serving plate. Cover with foil to keep warm.

To make remaining omelet, add *½ teaspoon* cooking oil to the hot skillet. Spread oil evenly by tilting and rotating the skillet. Cook and fill as above. Sprinkle cheese over omelets. Serves 2.

Chicken and Artichoke Omelets

1 cup skim milk
1 tablespoon cornstarch
1 tablespoon Dijon-style mustard
¼ teaspoon dried tarragon, crushed
1 9-ounce package frozen artichoke hearts, cooked, drained, and cut up
1 cup diced cooked chicken
6 eggs
3 tablespoons water
½ teaspoon salt
⅛ teaspoon pepper
   Nonstick spray coating
1½ teaspoons cooking oil

248 calories per serving

For filling, in a saucepan combine skim milk and cornstarch. Cook and stir till thickened and bubbly, then cook and stir for 2 minutes more. Stir in mustard and tarragon. Stir in artichokes and chicken, then heat through. Keep warm.

(See omelet-making photos 1–5, pages 96–97.) To make omelets, in a bowl beat together eggs, water, salt, and pepper till combined but not frothy. Spray a 6- or 8-inch skillet with nonstick coating, then heat the skillet. Add *one-fourth* of the egg mixture, about ⅓ cup, then cook over medium heat. As eggs set, run a spatula around the edge of the skillet, lifting the eggs to allow uncooked portion to flow underneath. When eggs are set but still shiny, remove from the heat. Fill omelet with *one-fourth* of the filling and transfer to a warm serving plate. Cover with foil to keep warm.

To make *each* of the three remaining omelets, add *½ teaspoon* cooking oil to the hot skillet. Spread oil evenly by tilting and rotating the skillet. Cook and fill as above. Makes 4 servings.

Pizza Omelets

- 1 14½-ounce can peeled Italian-style tomatoes, cut up
- 1 tablespoon dried parsley flakes
- ½ teaspoon sugar
- ½ teaspoon dried basil, crushed
- ½ teaspoon dried oregano, crushed
- ½ of a 4-ounce package sliced pepperoni, halved
- 6 eggs
- 3 tablespoons water
- ½ teaspoon minced dried onion
- ½ teaspoon dried parsley flakes
- ¼ teaspoon garlic salt
  Dash pepper
  Nonstick spray coating
- 1½ teaspoons cooking oil
- ¼ cup grated Parmesan cheese

256 calories per serving

For filling, in a medium saucepan mix *undrained* tomatoes, 1 tablespoon parsley flakes, sugar, basil, and oregano. Bring mixture to boiling. Add pepperoni. Reduce the heat and simmer, uncovered, for 10 to 12 minutes or till slightly thickened.

(See omelet-making photos 1–5, pages 96–97.) To make omelets, in a bowl beat together eggs, water, onion, ½ teaspoon parsley flakes, garlic salt, and pepper till combined but not frothy. Spray a 6- or 8-inch skillet with nonstick coating, then heat the skillet. Add *one-fourth* of the egg mixture, about ⅓ cup, then cook over medium heat. As eggs set, run a spatula around edge of the skillet, lifting the eggs to allow uncooked portion to flow underneath. When eggs are set but still shiny, remove from the heat. Reserve about ⅓ cup of the filling. Fill omelet with *one-fourth* of the remaining filling and transfer to a warm plate. Cover with foil to keep warm.

To make *each* of the three remaining omelets, add ½ *teaspoon* cooking oil to the hot skillet. Spread oil evenly by tilting and rotating the skillet. Cook and fill as above. Top omelets with reserved filling and cheese. Serves 4.

Greek Omelets

Feta cheese, pronounced (FEHT-ah), is white and crumbly with a salty flavor.

- 1 10-ounce package frozen chopped spinach
- 8 eggs
- ¼ cup water
- ¼ teaspoon salt
- ¼ teaspoon ground nutmeg
- ⅛ teaspoon onion powder
- ⅛ teaspoon pepper
  Nonstick spray coating
- ½ cup crumbled feta cheese (2 ounces)
- 1½ teaspoons cooking oil
- ¼ cup plain low-fat yogurt

241 calories per serving

For filling, in a medium saucepan cook spinach according to package directions; drain in colander. Squeeze out the excess liquid by pressing the spinach against the colander with the back of a wooden spoon. Keep warm.

(See omelet-making photos 1–5, pages 96–97.) To make omelets, in a bowl beat together eggs, water, salt, nutmeg, onion powder, and pepper till combined but not frothy. Spray a 6- or 8-inch skillet with nonstick coating, then heat the skillet. Add *one-fourth* of the egg mixture, about ½ cup, then cook over medium heat. As eggs set, run a spatula around edge of the skillet, lifting the eggs to allow uncooked portion to flow underneath. When eggs are set but still shiny, remove from the heat. Spoon about *one-fourth* of the filling across the center. Sprinkle with *one-fourth* of the feta cheese. Fold omelet and transfer to a warm serving plate. Cover with foil to keep warm.

To make *each* of the three remaining omelets, add ½ *teaspoon* oil to the hot skillet. Spread oil evenly by tilting and rotating the skillet. Cook and fill as above. Dollop omelets with yogurt. Makes 4 servings.

Classic Crepes

Crepes, those deliciously thin pancakes, add flair to any meal. By trimming the cooking oil and reducing the number of eggs, we've created a crepe recipe that's a calorie-counter's delight. Fill regular or whole wheat crepes with any one of five scrumptious fillings.

Cheesy Ham-Filled Crepes

Calorie Counter's Crepes

1½ cups skim milk
1 cup all-purpose flour *or* whole
    wheat flour
1 egg
1 egg white
   Nonstick spray coating

38 calories per crepe

In a bowl combine milk, flour, egg, and egg white. Beat with a rotary beater till blended. Spray a 6-inch skillet with nonstick coating. Place over medium heat till a drop of water sizzles (see photo 1). Remove from heat. Spoon in *2 tablespoons* batter. Tilt skillet to spread batter (see photo 2). Return to heat, then brown on one side, about 1 minute. (*Or,* cook on an inverted crepe pan.) Run a metal spatula around edge of crepe to loosen. Invert skillet and remove crepe (see photo 3). Lightly greasing skillet occasionally, repeat to make 18 crepes.

1 Heat the skillet over medium heat. Sprinkle a few drops of water on the hot surface. If the water sizzles, as shown, the skillet is ready to use.

    When making the remaining crepes, nonstick coating will not work on the hot skillet—grease lightly with cooking oil or shortening instead.

2 Pour *2 tablespoons* of the crepe batter into the heated skillet. Lift and tilt the skillet, as shown, so the batter covers the pan in a thin, even layer. If the batter won't swirl to coat, thin the batter in the bowl with a little water and refill the skillet. If there's a tear in the crepe or a bubble breaks leaving a hole, patch it with a little extra batter.

Cheesy Ham-Filled Crepes

8 Calorie Counter's Crepes
   (see recipe, left)
1 10-ounce package frozen chopped
   broccoli
1 cup skim milk
1 tablespoon cornstarch
½ cup shredded American cheese
   (2 ounces)
1 teaspoon prepared mustard
4 ounces fully cooked ham, finely
   chopped (¾ cup)
1 2½-ounce jar sliced
   mushrooms, drained
   Snipped chives

238 calories per serving

Prepare crepes (see photos 1–3). Set aside. Cook broccoli according to package directions. Drain and set aside. In saucepan mix milk and cornstarch. Cook and stir till thickened and bubbly. Add cheese and mustard, then cook and stir till cheese is melted. Reserve *½ cup* sauce.

For filling, stir broccoli, ham, and mushrooms into remaining sauce, then heat through. Spoon about *⅓ cup* filling down the center of each crepe, then fold the sides over (see photo 4). Arrange crepes in a 12x7½x2-inch baking dish. Pour reserved sauce over crepes. Bake, covered, in a 350° oven for 15 to 20 minutes. Sprinkle chives over crepes. Makes 4 servings.

3 Invert the crepe over paper towels, as shown. Let the crepe fall, then smooth it out, if necessary, so that the crepe lies flat.

4 Spoon the filling along the center of the un-browned side of the crepe, as shown. Fold two sides of the crepe to the center so they overlap.

Stacked Shrimp Creole

8 **Calorie Counter's Crepes (see recipe, page 102)**
¾ **pound fresh *or* frozen shelled shrimp**
1 **16-ounce can tomatoes, cut up**
½ **cup chopped onion**
½ **cup chopped green pepper**
½ **cup chopped celery**
1 **clove garlic, minced**
1 **bay leaf**
½ **teaspoon salt**
½ **teaspoon dried thyme, crushed**
⅛ **teaspoon ground red pepper**
4 **teaspoons cornstarch**
2 **tablespoons snipped parsley**

216 calories per serving

Prepare crepes (see photos 1–3, pages 102–103). Set aside. Thaw shrimp, if frozen. In a 10-inch skillet combine *undrained* tomatoes, next eight ingredients, and ¼ cup *water*. Cover and simmer for 15 minutes or till celery is tender. Stir together cornstarch and 2 tablespoons cold *water,* then add to tomato mixture. Cook and stir till thickened and bubbly. Stir in shrimp, and return to boiling. Cover and simmer for 5 minutes or till shrimp are done. Remove bay leaf.

Place one crepe, brown side up, on a plate. Top with ½ *cup* shrimp mixture, then another crepe and ½ *cup* shrimp mixture. Repeat to make four stacks. Sprinkle with parsley. Serves 4.

Freezing Crepes

Keep extra crepes on hand by freezing them. Stack crepes alternately with two layers of waxed paper. Pack the stack in a moisture- and vaporproof bag. Freeze for up to four months.

Sweet-Sour Pork Crepes

8 **Calorie Counter's Crepes (see recipe, page 102)**
¾ **pound lean boneless pork**
 Nonstick spray coating
½ **cup chopped green pepper**
1 **clove garlic, minced**
½ **cup finely shredded carrot**
¼ **cup sugar**
¼ **cup white wine vinegar**
1 **teaspoon instant beef bouillon granules**
1 **teaspoon soy sauce**
2 **tablespoons cornstarch**
 Snipped parsley

267 calories per serving

Prepare crepes (see photos 1–3, pages 102–103). Set aside. Trim separable fat from pork (see photo 1, page 24). Partially freeze pork. Thinly slice across the grain into bite-size strips (see photo 1, page 60). Spray a 10-inch skillet with nonstick coating, then heat. Add pork, green pepper, and garlic. Cook, stirring occasionally, till pork is no longer pink.

In a small saucepan mix carrot, sugar, vinegar, bouillon granules, soy sauce, and 1 cup *water,* then bring to boiling. Combine ⅓ cup cold *water* and cornstarch. Add to carrot mixture. Cook and stir till thickened and bubbly, then cook and stir for 2 minutes more. Reserve ½ *cup* sauce. Stir remaining sauce into pork mixture.

Spoon about ¼ *cup* filling down the center of each crepe, then fold sides over (see photo 4, page 103). Arrange crepes in a 12x7½x2-inch baking dish, then top with reserved sauce. Bake, covered, in a 350° oven for 15 to 20 minutes or till heated through. Trim with parsley. Serves 4.

Turkey Crepes

Splurge with a dollop of cranberry sauce. It's well worth the few extra calories.

8 **Calorie Counter's Crepes (see recipe, page 102)**
1 **small apple, cored and chopped**
⅓ **cup chopped celery**
2 **tablespoons chopped onion**
2 **tablespoons snipped parsley**
2 **tablespoons water**
½ **teaspoon salt**
¼ **teaspoon poultry seasoning**
⅛ **teaspoon pepper**
1¼ **cups skim milk**
4 **teaspoons cornstarch**
2 **cups diced cooked turkey *or* chicken**
Cranberry sauce (optional)

280 calories per serving

Prepare crepes (see photos 1–3, pages 102–103). Set aside. In a small saucepan combine apple, celery, onion, parsley, water, salt, poultry seasoning, and pepper. Cook, covered, for 5 to 6 minutes or till vegetables are tender. Drain. Stir together milk and cornstarch, then add to the saucepan. Cook and stir till thickened and bubbly, then cook and stir for 2 minutes more. Reserve *½ cup* sauce.

Stir turkey or chicken into remaining sauce and heat through. Spoon about *¼ cup* turkey mixture down the center of each crepe, then fold sides over (see photo 4, page 103). Arrange crepes in a 12x7½x2-inch baking dish. Pour the reserved sauce over crepes. Bake, covered, in a 350° oven for 15 to 20 minutes or till heated through. Dollop crepes with cranberry sauce, if desired. Makes 4 servings.

Beef Stroganoff Cups

Crepe cups are a fun twist on the traditional roll-up.

4 **Calorie Counter's Crepes (see recipe, page 102)**
Nonstick spray coating
¾ **pound beef top round steak**
1 **tablespoon cooking oil**
1 **cup sliced fresh mushrooms**
¼ **cup finely chopped onion**
½ **cup beef broth**
½ **cup dairy sour cream**
1 **tablespoon all-purpose flour**
Parsley sprigs

220 calories per serving

Prepare crepes (see photos 1–3, pages 102–103). Invert four custard cups on a baking sheet, then spray with nonstick coating. Place one crepe, brown side up, on top of each cup. Press crepe over cup, pinching to form three or four pleats. Bake in a 375° oven for 20 minutes or till crisp. Remove from the oven and cool.

Trim separable fat from meat (see photo 1, page 24). Partially freeze meat. Thinly slice meat across the grain into bite-size strips (see photo 1, page 60). Preheat a wok or skillet over high heat and add cooking oil. Stir-fry mushrooms and onion for 2 to 3 minutes. Transfer vegetables to a bowl. Stir-fry meat for 3 to 4 minutes (see photo 5, page 91). Push meat from center of wok, then add beef broth to center of wok. Stir together sour cream and flour and stir into beef broth. Cook and stir till thickened and bubbly, then cook and stir for 1 minute more. Return vegetables to wok. Cover and cook 1 minute. Spoon mixture into crepe cups. Garnish with parsley. Makes 4 servings.

Satisfying Dinner Pies

A dieter's dream come true, these dinner pies feature a low-calorie pastry crust that substitutes cottage cheese for some of the fat in regular pastry. The result—a crisp crust with a whole wheat texture and appearance.

Terrific Taco Pie

Calorie-Trimmed Pastry

⅓ cup low-fat cream-style cottage cheese
1 cup all-purpose flour
¼ teaspoon salt
3 tablespoons shortening
2 to 3 tablespoons cold water

143 calories for ⅙ of pastry

Push cottage cheese through a sieve with a spoon (see photo 1). In a bowl stir together flour and salt. Cut in shortening till pieces are the size of small peas (see photo 2). Add cottage cheese to flour mixture and combine with a fork. Sprinkle *1 tablespoon* cold water over part of the mixture. Toss with a fork. Push to the side of the bowl. Repeat with remaining water till all is moistened. Form into a ball (see photo 3).

On a lightly floured surface flatten dough with hands. Roll from center to edge, forming a 12-inch circle (see photo 4). Wrap around a rolling pin. Unroll into a 9-inch pie plate (see photo 5). Ease pastry into pie plate (do not stretch). Trim to ½ inch beyond edge of plate. Fold under extra pastry. Flute edge (see photo 6). Fill and bake as directed. Makes 1 (9-inch) shell.

Terrific Taco Pie

Calorie-Trimmed Pastry
   (see recipe, left)
1 pound lean ground beef
½ cup chopped onion
¼ cup chopped green pepper
1 clove garlic, minced
1 8-ounce can tomato sauce
½ to 1 teaspoon chili powder
½ cup taco sauce
1 tablespoon cornstarch
½ cup shredded American cheese
1½ cups shredded lettuce
½ of a medium tomato, chopped

367 calories per serving

Prepare pastry shell and line with heavy foil (see photo 7). Bake in a 450° oven about 15 minutes or till light brown. Carefully remove foil. Reduce the oven temperature to 350°. In a 10-inch skillet cook beef, onion, green pepper, and garlic till meat is brown. Drain off fat. Stir in tomato sauce and chili powder. Stir together taco sauce and cornstarch. Stir into skillet; cook and stir till bubbly. Turn into pastry shell. Bake for 15 minutes. Sprinkle cheese over pie. Let stand for 5 minutes. Top with lettuce and tomato. Serves 6.

1 Working over a mixing bowl, use the back of a wooden spoon to push the cottage cheese through a sieve, as shown.

2 Use a pastry blender to cut shortening into the flour mixture till pieces are the size of small peas, as shown. Or, use two knives and cut through the mixture with a crossing motion.
   The key to light, flaky pastry is to avoid blending the shortening completely with the flour.

3 Moisten all of the flour mixture with water, then use a fork to form the dough into a ball, as shown. Use your hands to help shape the ball.

4 Flatten pastry with your hands and smooth the edges. Roll the dough with a rolling pin from the center to the edges with light, even strokes, forming a 12-inch circle.

5 Loosely unroll the pastry into a 9-inch pie plate, as shown. Avoid stretching the pastry, or it will shrink as it bakes.

6 Flute the edge of the pastry by pressing the dough between two index fingers, as shown, or with the forefinger of one hand against the thumb and forefinger of the other hand. This gives a decorative edge and helps reduce shrinkage.

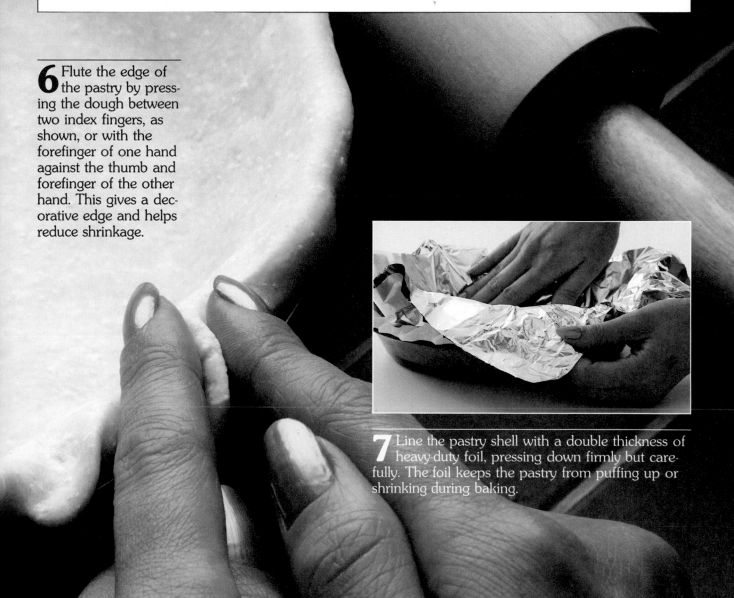

7 Line the pastry shell with a double thickness of heavy-duty foil, pressing down firmly but carefully. The foil keeps the pastry from puffing up or shrinking during baking.

Pork Pot Pie

It's your choice—leftover pork, chicken, beef, turkey, and ham work equally well in this savory pie.

Calorie-Trimmed Pastry (see recipe, page 108)
1   10-ounce package frozen peas and carrots
1   cup water
½   cup chopped celery
½   cup chopped onion
¼   cup snipped parsley
3   tablespoons cornstarch
2   teaspoons instant chicken bouillon granules
¼   teaspoon salt
¼   teaspoon ground sage
¼   teaspoon dried thyme, crushed
⅛   teaspoon pepper
1   cup skim milk
2   cups cubed cooked pork

321 calories per serving

Prepare pastry, *except* roll into a 12x8-inch rectangle (see photos 1–4, pages 108–109). Set aside. In a large saucepan cook peas and carrots, water, celery, onion, and parsley for 5 to 8 minutes or till celery is tender. In a bowl stir together cornstarch, bouillon granules, salt, sage, thyme, and pepper, then stir in milk. Stir into vegetable mixture. Cook and stir till thickened and bubbly. Stir in pork and heat through.

Turn hot mixture into a 10x6x2-inch baking dish. Place pastry over filling. Crimp pastry against edge of dish. Cut slits for escape of steam. Bake in a 425° oven for 25 to 30 minutes or till top is light brown. Let stand for 10 minutes before serving. Makes 6 servings.

Chicken-Chili Pepper Quiche

Calorie-Trimmed Pastry (see recipe, page 108)
3   slightly beaten eggs
1¼   cups evaporated skim milk
1   cup shredded Monterey Jack cheese (4 ounces)
¾   cup chopped cooked chicken *or* turkey
1   4-ounce can diced green chili peppers, rinsed and drained
½   teaspoon salt
⅛   teaspoon pepper
    Several dashes bottled hot pepper sauce
1   medium tomato, sliced
    Parsley sprigs (optional)

334 calories per serving

Prepare pastry shell (see photos 1–6, pages 108–109). Line pastry shell with heavy foil (see photo 7, page 109). Bake in a 450° oven about 15 minutes or till light brown. Carefully remove foil. Reduce the oven temperature to 325°.

Meanwhile, in a large bowl combine eggs, milk, Monterey Jack cheese, chicken or turkey, chili peppers, salt, pepper, and hot pepper sauce. Pour into baked pastry shell.

Bake in the 325° oven for 35 to 40 minutes or till a knife inserted near the center comes out clean. Remove from the oven, then top with tomato slices. Let stand for 10 minutes before serving. Garnish with parsley sprigs, if desired. Makes 6 servings.

Ham and Cheese Quiche

When we say cheese, we mean cheese! This delicate quiche has cottage cheese in the crust and two kinds of cheese in the filling.

Calorie-Trimmed Pastry (see recipe, page 108)
1 **cup low-fat cottage cheese**
1 **cup skim milk**
3 **eggs**
1 **tablespoon all-purpose flour**
   Dash ground nutmeg
1 **cup diced fully cooked ham**
1 **cup shredded Swiss cheese (4 ounces)**
2 **tablespoons thinly sliced green onion**

351 calories per serving

Prepare pastry shell (see photos 1–6, pages 108–109). Line pastry shell with heavy foil (see photo 7, page 109). Bake in a 450° oven about 15 minutes or till light brown. Carefully remove foil. Reduce the oven temperature to 325°.

Meanwhile, in a blender container or food processor bowl combine cottage cheese, milk, eggs, flour, and nutmeg. Cover, then blend or process till smooth. Stir in ham, Swiss cheese, and onion. Pour into baked pastry shell. Bake in the 325° oven for 45 to 50 minutes or till a knife inserted near the center comes out clean. Let stand for 10 minutes before serving. Serves 6.

Lamb-Eggplant Pie

As the pie bakes, the creamy, cheesy topping puffs up slightly.

Calorie-Trimmed Pastry (see recipe, page 108)
1 **pound ground lamb *or* lean ground beef**
½ **cup chopped onion**
2 **cups peeled, chopped eggplant**
1 **8-ounce can stewed tomatoes, cut up**
¼ **cup snipped parsley**
½ **teaspoon salt**
¼ **teaspoon dry mustard**
¼ **teaspoon pepper**
1 **tablespoon cold water**
2 **teaspoons cornstarch**
1 **slightly beaten egg**
1 **cup low-fat cottage cheese**
½ **cup shredded mozzarella cheese (2 ounces)**

332 calories per serving

Prepare pastry shell (see photos 1–6, pages 108–109). Line pastry shell with heavy foil (see photo 7, page 109). Bake in a 450° oven about 15 minutes or till light brown. Carefully remove foil. Reduce the oven temperature to 400°.

In a 10-inch skillet cook meat and onion till meat is brown. Drain off fat. Stir in eggplant, *undrained* tomatoes, parsley, salt, mustard, and pepper. Bring to boiling and reduce heat. Cover and simmer for 5 to 7 minutes or till eggplant is tender. Stir together water and cornstarch, then add to the meat mixture. Cook and stir till thickened and bubbly. Turn into baked pastry shell.

In a small bowl combine egg, cottage cheese, and mozzarella cheese. Spread over meat mixture. Bake in the 400° oven for 18 to 20 minutes. Cover edges with foil for the last few minutes of baking to prevent overbrowning, if necessary. Let stand for 10 minutes before serving. Makes 6 servings.

Saltimbocca Dinner

Company's coming! When dinner guests arrive at the door, diet plans often go out the window. Keep everybody happy with this delightful low-calorie dinner for four. Assemble the entire meal in less than 1½ hours.

Menu

416 calories per serving

- Slimming Saltimbocca*
- Broccoli Spears
- Garden Salad*
- Breadsticks
- Strawberries with Strawberry Sauce*

*see pages 114-117

Slimming Saltimbocca

Slimming Saltimbocca

1 **pound veal leg round *or* sirloin steak, cut ¼ inch thick**
Salt
Pepper
2 **slices boiled ham, halved (2 ounces)**
1 **slice mozzarella cheese, quartered (1½ ounces)**
½ **teaspoon ground sage**
3 **tablespoons fine dry bread crumbs**
2 **tablespoons snipped parsley *or* 2 teaspoons dried parsley flakes**
¼ **teaspoon paprika (optional)**
2 **tablespoons skim milk**

220 calories per serving

Trim separable fat from meat (see photo 1, page 24). Cut into four equal pieces (see photo 1). With the smooth side of a meat mallet pound each piece into a rectangle about ⅛ inch thick (see photo 2). Sprinkle lightly with salt and pepper. Place *half* of a ham slice and a *quarter* of a cheese slice on each piece of meat. Sprinkle with sage. Fold in sides, then roll up jelly-roll style (see photo 3). Secure meat rolls with wooden toothpicks.

In a bowl mix bread crumbs, parsley, and paprika, if desired. Dip rolls in milk, then roll in crumb mixture (see photo 4). Place seam side down in a shallow baking dish. Bake in a 350° oven for 35 to 40 minutes or till done. Serves 4.

1 Using a sharp knife, cut the steak into four equal pieces. By making the pieces as uniform as possible, you can make sure everyone receives the same portion size and number of calories.

2 Using the smooth side of a meat mallet, gently pound each piece of meat into a rectangle, working from the center to the edges, until the meat is ⅛ inch thick.

3 Place the ham and then the cheese on each piece of meat. Sprinkle sage evenly over the ham and cheese. Fold in the sides. This helps prevent the melting cheese from oozing out. Roll up the meat jelly-roll style. Secure with wooden toothpicks, if necessary.

4 Dip the meat rolls, one at a time, first in the milk (to moisten the surface) and then in the crumb mixture. Roll them around in the mixture to make sure they are well coated. Place the coated meat rolls in a baking dish or pan, seam side down.

Timetable

1¼ hrs. before
● Start preparing the Slimming Saltimbocca. Place it in the oven 40 minutes before serving time.

30 mins. before
● Prepare the strawberry sauce and yogurt mixture for the dessert. Place them in the refrigerator to chill. Cut up the strawberries. Cover and chill.

15 mins. before
● Start cooking the broccoli. While the broccoli cooks, arrange the breadsticks in a basket.
● Prepare the Garden Salad.

At Serving Time
● Add the dressing to the salad and toss. Place the salad in salad bowls and sprinkle with cheese. Drain the broccoli and place it in a serving bowl.
● Swirl the strawberry sauce and yogurt mixture together on individual dessert plates. Top it with the strawberries. Chill till dessert time.

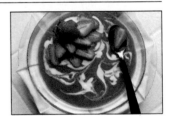

Strawberries with Strawberry Sauce

3 cups fresh *or* frozen unsweetened
   strawberries
2 tablespoons honey
2 tablespoons brandy *or* rum
¼ cup plain low-fat yogurt
1 tablespoon sifted powdered sugar

104 calories per serving

If using fresh strawberries, wash berries and drain, then remove hulls. Thaw strawberries, if frozen. Reserve 16 strawberries (about 1 cup). In a food processor bowl or blender container combine remaining strawberries, honey, and brandy. Cover and process or blend till smooth. Transfer to a bowl. Cover and chill. In a small bowl mix yogurt and sugar. Cover and chill. Slice reserved berries, reserving four whole berries for garnish.

To serve, spoon strawberry sauce onto shallow dessert plates. Swirl some of the yogurt mixture through sauce. Arrange sliced berries atop. Garnish with whole strawberries. Serves 4.

Garden Salad

See photo, page 112.

2 cups torn salad greens
1 medium tomato, cut into wedges
½ cup sliced radishes
½ of a small cucumber *or* zucchini
¼ cup reduced-calorie blue cheese
   salad dressing
2 tablespoons grated Parmesan cheese

38 calories per serving

In a bowl combine torn greens, tomato, and radishes. Run a fork lengthwise down cucumber or zucchini to score it. Cut into ⅛-inch slices, then add to salad. Add salad dressing; toss gently to coat. Spoon salad into individual salad bowls. Sprinkle with cheese. Makes 4 servings.

Tomatoes Vinaigrette

A quick-to-fix alternative to Garden Salad.

4 medium tomatoes
½ cup sliced fresh mushrooms
1 tablespoon sliced green onion
⅓ cup reduced-calorie Italian
   salad dressing
   Lettuce

40 calories per serving

Peel tomatoes, if desired. Cut into wedges. Place tomatoes, mushrooms, and onion into a bowl. Pour dressing over vegetables. Cover and chill about 4 hours. Stir once or twice. Before serving, line individual salad plates with lettuce. Remove vegetables from dressing with a slotted spoon and arrange on lettuce. Drizzle with dressing. Makes 4 servings.

Orange Fluff

A great make-ahead dessert option.

½ teaspoon finely shredded orange peel
1 cup orange juice
2 teaspoons unflavored gelatin
⅛ teaspoon ground nutmeg
1 egg white
½ of a 4-ounce carton (scant 1 cup) frozen
   whipped topping, thawed

85 calories per serving

In a small saucepan combine orange peel, orange juice, gelatin, and nutmeg. Let stand for 5 minutes. Heat and stir till gelatin dissolves. Remove from the heat. Chill mixture till partially set. In a small mixer bowl beat egg white with an electric mixer till foamy. Gradually add gelatin mixture, beating at high speed till fluffy, 1 to 2 minutes. Fold in topping. (Chill till mixture mounds, if necessary.) Spoon into four dessert dishes. Chill till set. Makes 4 servings.

1 cup strawberries with
¼ cup half-and-half
and 1 teaspoon
powdered sugar
146 calories

Lettuce wedge with 1
tablespoon Thousand
Island salad dressing
92 calories

½ cup cooked green
and wax beans with 1
tablespoon butter
132 calories

1 medium baked potato
with 1 tablespoon
sour cream and 1
slice cooked bacon,
crumbled
214 calories

Fried chicken breast half
with skin (4 ounces)
234 calories

818 calories

Calorie Countdown

Every dieter longs to unlock the secret of successful dieting: cutting calories, but not fresh flavors and toothsome taste. Impossible, you say? Just look at the example above and you'll see how easy it is to cleverly trim calories. Look even closer and you'll see that what you reduce is calories, not the good taste of the food you enjoy.

Why lose weight?
Aside from the desire for an improved personal appearance, why should you take a look at shedding extra pounds? It's estimated that half of all American adults are overweight or obese. This excess body fat puts unnecessary strain on the joints, vital organs, and respiratory and circulatory systems. Obese people also tend to have a higher incidence of high blood pressure and diabetes.

The big C—calories
So, what are calories? Calories are much more than just a number attached to a portion of food. Calories are units that measure the amount of energy your body receives from the food you eat. Here's how they work.

For every 3,500 calories you consume, your body stores one pound of fat, or energy. When you use fewer calories than your body takes in, you gain weight. And when you use more calories than you consume, you lose weight.

1 cup strawberries with
  ¼ cup skim milk
77 calories

Lettuce wedge with
  1 tablespoon diet
  Thousand Island
  salad dressing
39 calories

½ cup cooked green
  and wax beans
30 calories

1 medium baked potato
  with 1 tablespoon
  plain yogurt
  and snipped chives
152 calories

Roasted or baked
  chicken breast half
  without skin
  (4 ounces)
206 calories

504 calories

Enough is enough!
Well, how can you tell when you've had enough calories? To determine your calorie needs, first calculate how many calories your body needs each day to maintain its current weight (multiply your present weight by 15). Then determine how many calories you need to eliminate from your diet each day in order to lose weight (subtract either 500 or 1,000 calories from the number needed to maintain your present weight). By subtracting 500 calories, you can expect to lose about 1 pound a week, and by subtracting 1,000 calories, you can expect to lose about 2 pounds a week. It's hard to get the more than 40 nutrients your body needs daily by consuming less than 1,000 calories per day. So when dieting, try to keep your daily intake above 1,000 calories.

Keeping it off
No matter how much weight you lose, the real challenge is keeping it off. By making reasonable changes in your life-style, you can make your newfound weight loss a permanent one. Be sure to include some type of physical activity as a part of your daily routine.

Exercising
Exercise not only burns calories, but improves fitness and mental relaxation as well. Plan to get regular exercise rather than occasional strenuous activity. The best way to have a regular exercise program and stick with it is to tailor it to your individual life-style and needs. Even everyday chores like mowing the lawn, spading the garden, or shoveling snow offer exercise.

Before starting an exercise routine, make sure you are ready medically. When your doctor has given you the OK, plan to make exercise part of your daily routine. Whether you decide to jog, swim, or cycle, set a pace that's comfortable for you. Start any exercise off slowly. Exercise long enough to get a good workout, but not so long that you feel fatigued. Then, slowly increase the time you spend exercising. The reward of a healthier, leaner body will be worth the effort.

**Milk-Cheese
Group**

**Bread-Cereal
Group**

Slimming Success

Variety is the spice of life! So why not make it the spice of your diet as well? The Five Basic Food Groups allow you to make choices in your food selection without time-consuming calculations. Choose the proper number of servings from each category and you'll be sure to receive all the nutrients you need each day.

Variety, the spice of diet!

Even when you're counting calories, it's easy to make meals extra special. Learning how to combine different types of food can add a world of variety to your meals. Planning your meals around the Five Basic Food Groups allows you plenty of flexibility. The five food groups are: Milk-Cheese; Bread-Cereal; Vegetable-Fruit; Meat, Poultry, Fish, Nuts, and Beans; and Fats, Sweets, and Alcohol. When choosing foods from each category, keep these calorie-conscious tips in mind.

Milk-Cheese Group

The foods in this group contain calcium, riboflavin, protein, and vitamins A, B_6, and B_{12}. Choose dairy products made with skim or low-fat milk.

Recommended daily servings: Plan three servings for children 9 to 12, four for teens, two for adults, three for pregnant women, and four for nursing mothers.

A serving is 1 cup of skim milk, 1 cup of low-fat yogurt, 2 cups of cottage cheese, ¼ cup of Parmesan cheese, or 1½ cups of ice milk.

Vegetable-Fruit
Group

Meat, Poultry,
Fish, Nuts, and
Beans Group

Bread-Cereal Group

This group of foods includes breads, pasta, and a selection of whole grain products. Look for whole grain or enriched breads and pastas. Many breakfast cereals are fortified with needed nutrients.

Recommended daily servings: Plan four servings from this group each day.

A serving is 1 slice of whole grain bread, ½ cup of cooked cereal, macaroni, noodles, or rice, or 1 ounce of ready-to-eat cereal.

Vegetable-Fruit Group

Fruits and vegetables provide vitamins A and C and fiber. With the exception of avocados and olives, all fruits and vegetables are naturally low in calories. Choose unsweetened fruits—fresh, frozen, canned, or dried. Fresh fruits are best because they are more filling than other options.

Recommended daily servings: Plan four servings daily.

A serving is ½ cup of any fruit or vegetable or 1 medium orange, apple, or baked potato, or a lettuce wedge.

Meat, Poultry, Fish, Nuts, and Beans Group

Control calories by remembering that your body needs only 6 ounces of meat a day. Fish and poultry are best for calorie counters because they have less fat. Lean meats cooked without added fat also work well. Occasionally include dried beans and peas for variety.

Recommended daily servings: Plan two servings daily, but be sure to vary the source.

A serving is 2 to 3 ounces of lean, cooked meat, 2 eggs, 1 cup of cooked dried beans, peas, or soybeans, 2 tablespoons of peanut butter, or ¼ to ½ cup of nuts, sesame seeds, or sunflower seeds.

Fats, Sweets, and Alcohol Group

Mayonnaise, candy, sugar, soft drinks, and alcoholic beverages fall into this category. Because they are high in calories—but low in minerals, vitamins, and protein—they provide little or no nutritional value. Try to minimize foods in this category. Use of these foods in your diet depends on the number of calories you can afford to consume.

Nutrition Analysis Chart

Use these analyses to compare nutritional values of different recipes. This information was calculated using Agriculture Handbook Number 456, published by the United States Department of Agriculture, as the primary source.

In compiling the nutrition analyses, we made the following assumptions:
- For all of the main-dish meat recipes, the nutrition analyses were calculated using weights or measures for cooked lean meat.

- Garnishes and optional ingredients were not included in the nutrition analyses.
- If a marinade was brushed over the food during cooking, the analysis includes all of the marinade.
- When two ingredient options appear in a recipe, calculations were made using the first one.
- For ingredients of variable weight (such as "2½- to 3-pound broiler-fryer chicken") or for recipes with a serving range ("makes 1 to 6 servings"), calculations were made using the first figure.

	Per Serving						Percent USRDA Per Serving							
	Calories	Protein (g)	Carbohydrate (g)	Fat (g)	Sodium (mg)	Potassium (mg)	Protein	Vitamin A	Vitamin C	Thiamine	Riboflavin	Niacin	Calcium	Iron
Main Dishes, Beef														
Beef Eater's Bounty (p. 20)	203	17	10	11	315	525	27	37	35	9	23	17	14	17
Beef Stroganoff Cups (p. 105)	220	16	11	12	125	310	25	5	3	9	18	19	7	11
Beefy Borscht (p. 38)	150	17	9	5	667	461	26	27	52	5	11	14	5	15
Beefy Vegetable-Sauced Pasta (p. 57)	305	24	32	9	663	804	37	41	127	22	19	33	5	29
Burgundy Beef (p. 26)	176	22	7	4	68	393	33	61	7	5	11	21	3	16
Cheese-Stuffed Burgers (p. 51)	245	28	4	13	251	351	42	10	11	8	17	27	8	20
Lemon-Marinated Steak (p. 81)	158	21	1	7	127	248	32	1	10	4	9	20	1	14
Orange-Beef Stir-Fry (p. 92)	183	21	19	4	710	717	32	62	257	16	24	22	15	20
Pepper Steak (p. 60)	229	21	25	5	826	417	32	10	99	14	15	22	3	19
Quick Beef Stew (p. 62)	249	25	25	6	919	568	38	20	36	10	16	29	4	20
Roast Beef with Mushroom Sauce (p. 75)	163	25	2	5	308	302	39	0	5	13	25	1	17	0
Roast Eye of Round with Vegetables (p. 74)	169	19	10	6	81	345	30	9	19	6	12	18	4	17
Saucy Steaks (p. 27)	300	22	29	10	570	256	35	9	4	11	15	21	10	15
Sesame Veal (p. 93)	289	25	8	17	178	562	38	27	58	14	21	30	4	19
Sherry-Marinated Steaks (p. 78)	164	21	4	4	84	287	33	4	6	4	12	22	2	16
Slimming Saltimbocca (p. 114)	220	23	5	11	383	261	36	4	5	9	15	20	11	15
South Seas Steak Pinwheels (p. 51)	160	17	16	3	42	507	26	28	114	6	11	18	3	15
Spicy Beef Stew (p. 24)	160	18	15	4	526	673	28	172	109	11	16	20	8	17
Taco-Filled Zucchini Shells (p. 33)	191	20	6	10	198	465	30	15	46	8	16	23	11	16
Tangy Beef and Swiss Sandwiches (Whole Wheat Bread) (p. 12)	258	20	18	12	507	353	31	19	32	10	17	13	34	16
(Pita Bread) (p. 12)	230	19	12	11	356	280	30	19	32	8	16	10	32	13
(Tortillas) (p. 12)	285	20	22	13	356	280	31	19	32	5	20	14	36	17
Terrific Taco Pie (p. 108)	367	20	24	21	666	279	31	19	27	16	18	24	9	16

	Per Serving						Percent USRDA Per Serving							
	Calories	Protein (g)	Carbohydrate (g)	Fat (g)	Sodium (mg)	Potassium (mg)	Protein	Vitamin A	Vitamin C	Thiamine	Riboflavin	Niacin	Calcium	Iron
Main Dishes, Beef (continued)														
Veal à l'Orange (p. 75)	183	20	5	8	62	286	31	5	25	6	12	21	1	14
Veal Stew (p. 26)	221	19	20	8	314	847	29	146	89	13	17	27	7	21
Main Dishes, Eggs and Cheese														
Asparagus-Cheese Omelets (p. 96)	235	18	8	15	474	456	28	36	36	18	35	9	14	19
Cheese and Fruit Salad (p. 20)	285	14	27	15	451	283	21	20	12	5	17	2	41	7
Cheese and Veggie Sandwiches (Whole Wheat Bread) (p. 14)	188	16	22	5	523	376	24	47	45	10	15	7	12	10
(Tortillas) (p. 14)	215	16	25	6	373	303	24	47	44	5	18	8	14	11
Chicken and Artichoke Omelets (p. 98)	248	24	10	13	496	492	38	21	9	11	30	19	14	15
Egg Salad Surprise (Rye Bread) (p. 14)	293	17	20	17	511	539	27	39	53	14	22	7	21	19
(Pita Bread) (p. 14)	265	16	13	16	361	466	25	39	53	11	21	4	20	16
Eggs Olé (p. 42)	286	21	29	10	605	428	33	42	73	12	21	28	9	21
Greek Omelets (p. 99)	241	18	5	17	461	410	27	136	35	12	26	2	22	22
Pizza Omelets (p. 99)	256	6	18	10	658	378	25	40	35	12	20	7	13	15
Poached Eggs with Shrimp Sauce (p. 45)	194	19	7	10	361	419	29	128	35	9	21	5	23	21
Southwestern Omelets (p. 98)	259	17	9	17	468	320	27	49	96	11	24	5	18	18
Vegetable Carbonara (p. 54)	245	16	27	9	243	344	24	57	26	11	18	10	22	16
Vegetable-Tofu Soup (p. 39)	261	17	24	12	1110	423	25	79	17	12	21	7	39	15
Main Dishes, Fish and Seafood														
Crab with Lime Sauce (p. 87)	195	26	2	9	477	280	40	70	9	16	7	21	7	7
Fancy Fish Fillets (p. 80)	147	21	10	2	160	708	33	7	89	10	12	12	14	9
Fettuccine with Clam Sauce (p. 56)	238	15	33	5	625	367	23	64	16	20	22	14	24	24
Orange-Ginger Lobster (p. 50)	150	21	4	5	274	268	33	4	26	9	5	9	8	5
Pineapple-Sauced Fish (p. 81)	112	21	6	0	204	412	32	3	11	4	5	17	4	6
Poached Fish with Lemon-Dill Sauce (p. 45)	253	23	4	13	70	411	35	55	3	12	10	18	5	3
Poached Halibut in Tangy Lime Sauce (p. 44)	180	24	4	7	270	534	37	13	7	5	7	39	5	4
Salmon-Rice Bake (p. 8)	307	26	21	13	707	453	40	13	17	17	22	38	36	13
Scallops Italian (p. 56)	257	25	35		781	634	39	27	30	27	15	22	12	23
Seaside Sandwiches (Tortillas) (p. 15)	232	14	23	9	270	265	22	42	20	9	14	12	11	14
(Whole Wheat Bread) (p. 15)	205	14	19	8	420	337	22	42	20	14	11	11	9	13
Shellfish Soup (p. 38)	176	20	22	1	802	554	30	95	16	7	17	10	28	12
Shrimp and Spinach Stir-Fry (p. 93)	174	15	13	8	131	675	23	109	88	9	10	15	11	18
Spicy Steamed Fish (p. 84)	197	49	9	20	154	703	38	23	36	9	6	49	3	8
Stacked Shrimp Creole (p. 104)	216	23	27	2	599	675	35	28	84	15	16	23	14	17
Steamed Salmon with Horseradish Sauce (p. 86)	208	24	6	9	235	448	37	53	3	12	15	17	11	3
Steamed Snapper and Squash (p. 86)	251	25	21	7	480	472	38	14	36	21	6	6	4	10
Tempting Tuna Salad (p. 20)	213	22	8	10	436	349	34	40	63	7	18	33	21	12
Tropical Salmon Salad (p. 21)	237	25	13	9	591	568	39	6	29	8	17	47	27	9
Vegetable-Sauced Fish Fillets (p. 87)	201	29	7	5	424	570	44	44	5	8	13	15	12	6
Main Dishes, Lamb														
Greek-Style Stuffed Tomatoes (p. 32)	196	16	22	6	54	634	24	29	60	14	16	19	7	14
Lamb Chops and Vegetables (p. 27)	148	19	7	5	360	442	29	13	69	10	13	22	3	10
Lamb Chops with Lemon-Mustard Sauce (p. 48)	142	21	2	5	207	252	32	0	3	8	12	22	2	10
Lamb-Eggplant Pie (p. 111)	333	27	26	13	615	494	41	15	26	19	25	23	14	15

	Per Serving					Percent USRDA Per Serving								
	Calories	Protein (g)	Carbohydrate (g)	Fat (g)	Sodium (mg)	Potassium (mg)	Protein	Vitamin A	Vitamin C	Thiamine	Riboflavin	Niacin	Calcium	Iron
Main Dishes, Pork *(continued)*														
Oriental Soup (p. 36)	171	21	7	7	1172	351	32	8	18	38	17	24	2	18
Pineapple-Ham Kabobs (p. 50)	204	22	12	8	774	339	34	2	46	37	13	20	2	17
Pork-and-Spinach-Filled Vegetables (p. 30)	294	17	18	18	407	597	25	91	198	29	19	18	11	20
Pork and Zucchini Stir-Fry (p. 92)	234	20	10	13	784	547	31	83	24	49	21	28	5	19
Pork Pot Pie (p. 110)	321	20	29	14	499	388	31	93	20	35	21	21	9	17
Pork Roast Florentine (p. 72)	270	29	8	13	390	514	44	80	21	70	21	32	6	26
Pork Strips in Pineapple Sauce (p. 63)	245	18	24	9	116	519	28	89	31	35	16	20	6	18
Pork with Curry Relish (p. 74)	175	18	5	9	110	243	28	5	2	45	12	21	1	14
Sweet-Sour Pork Crepes (p. 104)	267	18	32	8	306	374	28	33	43	27	17	16	8	14
White Lasagna (p. 57)	284	26	26	8	623	434	41	29	59	30	30	16	30	12
Main Dishes, Poultry														
Brandied Tarragon Chicken (p. 69)	217	28	1	3	134	1	43	2	0	5	16	55	2	10
Carrot-Stuffed Chicken Rolls (p. 66)	214	29	10	5	185	359	45	164	14	8	15	56	6	13
Chicken-Barley Soup (p. 38)	126	16	10	3	713	303	24	56	6	4	7	23	3	7
Chicken-Chili Pepper Quiche (p. 110)	334	22	25	16	522	378	33	20	30	14	27	18	33	11
Chicken Parmesan (p. 68)	206	32	4	7	89	138	49	45	18	7	20	54	13	13
Curried Pinwheels (p. 69)	225	29	15	6	72	130	45	3	3	6	14	56	3	12
Curried Turkeywiches (Pita Bread) (p. 15)	261	22	22	8	134	311	34	8	29	9	11	23	5	10
(Tortillas) (p. 15)	276	21	24	10	134	311	33	8	29	4	14	26	7	13
Fruity Chicken Salad (p. 18)	184	22	14	5	287	698	33	89	98	10	18	30	12	17
Garlic Chicken (p. 90)	300	35	18	9	904	342	54	123	31	22	21	65	6	22
Ham-and-Cheese-Filled Chicken Rolls (p. 68)	267	37	4	11	499	153	57	9	6	21	21	59	4	18
Hawaiian Chicken (p. 44)	191	29	10	3	660	134	44	3	24	9	15	54	3	13
Hot Turkey Salad (p. 62)	154	19	9	5	337	373	30	75	70	8	17	29	8	17
Sausage and Cabbage Soup (p. 39)	215	13	14	0	526	406	4	3	79	6	4	5	4	3
Summer Fruit-Chicken Salad (p. 21)	241	20	27	6	185	651	32	29	26	7	15	31	6	11
Turkey Crepes (p. 105)	280	30	27	6	422	582	46	8	12	13	27	32	18	12
Turkey-Stuffed Tomato Shells (p. 33)	219	22	14	9	422	767	33	42	86	10	18	30	11	14
Turkey-Vegetable Casserole (p. 9)	247	13	30	9	431	171	7	51	7	6	4	8	3	8
Zesty Chicken (p. 44)	172	29	6	3	123	174	44	11	31	7	14	56	3	11
Miscellaneous														
Calorie Counter's Crepes (p. 102)	118	2	6	1	17	42	3	1	0	4	5	2	3	2
Calorie-Trimmed Pastry (p. 108)	143	4	16	7	140	32	6	0	9	6	6	1	4	4
Garden Salad (p. 117)	38	2	4	2	202	213	4	10	25	3	4	2	6	4
Orange Fluff (p. 117)	85	3	10	4	14	136	4	3	52	4	2	1	1	1
Salad Dressing Base (p. 18)	16	1	2	1	74	22	1	2	0	1	2	0	2	1
Strawberries with Strawberry Sauce (p. 117)	104	1	21	1	9	209	2	2	110	3	6	4	4	7
Tomatoes Vinaigrette (p. 117)	40	2	7	1	161	343	3	23	48	6	5	6	2	4

Tips

Have BETTER HOMES AND
GARDENS® magazine delivered
to your door. For information,
write to:
MR. ROBERT AUSTIN
P.O. BOX 4536
DES MOINES, IA 50336.